HOW TO DESIGN, ANALYZE, AND WRITE DOCTORAL RESEARCH

The Practical Guidebook

Edward S. Balian

UNIVERSITY
PRESS OF
AMERICA

LANHAM • NEW YORK • LONDON

CALIFORNIA SCHOOL OF PROFESSIONAL PSYCHOLOGY LOS ANGELES

Copyright © 1982 by

University Press of America,™ Inc.

4720 Boston Way
Lanham, MD 20706

3 Henrietta Street
London WC2E 8LU England

Library of Congress Cataloging in Publication Data

Balian, Edward S.
　How to design, analyze, and write doctoral research.

　　Includes index.
　　1. Dissertations, Academic–Handbooks, manuals,
etc. 2. Doctor of philosophy degree–Handbooks,
manuals, etc. 3. Report writing–Handbooks, manuals,
etc. 4. Research–Handbooks, manuals, etc. I. Title.
LB2386.B34　　　　1983　　808'.02　　　82–20164
ISBN 0–8191–2879–1
ISBN 0–8191–2880–5 (pbk.)

To Sarah and Ed

—Mom and Dad,

    Two very special and loving people.

Acknowledgements

The author wishes to thank the many individuals who helped make this book a reality. Foremost, regarding text content, much appreciation is extended to Alan Klaas, Ph.D., James Meznek, Ph.D., and Phyllis Yates, Ph.D., as their thoughtful suggestions proved extremely valuable.

Thanks are given to those at SPSS (Statistical Package for the Social Sciences), Chicago; ERIC (Educational Resource Index Center), Washington, D.C.; and Larry Nelson, Ph.D., author of the LERTAP computer program, University of Otago, Dunedin, New Zealand. Their fine cooperation allowed the text to be as comprehensive as possible.

The author acknowledges the Wayne State University staff at the Main Computing Center in Detroit for providing professional expertise and related services.

Gayle Green is thanked for the usual superb job in typing, layout, and editing, both in rough drafts and final manuscript. Her excellence in these capacities was unequaled by anyone, not to mention her coping skills in tolerating a very particular author.

Pat Kurth of Allen's Secretarial in Southfield, Michigan, is also thanked for her fine assistance in various typing services throughout the final manuscript. Peter Swanney of Word One, Incorporated in Bloomfield Hills, Michigan is thanked for the additional typing production of rough drafts.

Regarding the final manuscript proofreading and editing, Karen Obsniuk, Ph.D. is thanked for her thoughtful comments and suggestions. Artwork for the text was supplied by Mary Ann Skelton, and Martin Martlock is credited with the author photograph. Text photographs were supplied by Wayne State University, Detroit.

Michael Novak and Ronald Lombardi are thanked for their assistance in legal and accounting aspects, respectively.

The author further wishes to thank Alan Klaas, Ph.D. and John Camp, Ph.D. for their excellent support. Their personal and professional guidance and friendship over the years has been, and will continue to be, sincerely appreciated.

Appreciation is also extended to all the graduate students and private doctoral clients I have had the pleasure of instructing. Through their insightful questions and comments over the years, the basic content of this guidebook was slowly formulated.

Lastly, sincere thanks are given to my family and friends. Their outstanding support was equaled only by their patience and understanding throughout this entire project.

-Edward S. Balian, Ph.D.
September 1982

Table of Contents

                                                      Page

INTRODUCTION xvii

Chapter
   1. DEVELOPING RESEARCH IDEAS   1
       Introduction   1
       Developing a Final Workable Idea   3

   2. LITERATURE REVIEWS   15
       Introduction   15
       The Purpose of a Literature Review ...   15
       Journal Titles   15
       Searching in ERIC, Psychological
         Abstracts, and Related Document
         File Systems   16
       Reference Search Warnings   23
       Other Literature Review Sources
         and Search Methods   25
       How Many References Are Enough?   25
       The Literature Review Index Card
         System   26
       Summary   26

   3. UNDERSTANDING AND DEVELOPING
       HYPOTHESES   31

       Introduction   31
       Null Hypothesis   31
       Research Hypothesis   32
       Alternative (or Alternate)
         Hypothesis   33
       Directionality of Research
         Hypotheses   34
       Developing Null and Research
         Hypotheses   34
       Rejecting or Accepting the Null   39
       The Double-Whammy Syndrome and
         Directional Research Hypotheses   39
       Summary   39

Chapter   Page

   4. EVALUATING RESEARCH DESIGNS   43

       Introduction   43
       Understanding Experimental Research
         Designs   43
       Understanding Descriptive Research
         Designs   43
       Developing and Evaluating Your
         Research Design   44
       Summary   47

   5. INSTRUMENTATION AND TESTING   53

       Introduction   53
       Validity and Reliability
         Introduction   53
       Validity   55
       Acceptable Criterion-Related Validity
         Coefficients   58
       Reliability   60
       Item Analysis   66
       Selecting a Published Instrument   72
       Developing an Original Instrument   76
       Special Hazards in Instrumentation
         and Testing   85
       Pilot Testing   90
       Summary   91

   6. SAMPLING TECHNIQUES AND DATA
   COLLECTION METHODS   99

       Introduction   99
       Definitions   99
       Common Methods of Sampling   100
       Selecting the Optimal Sampling
         Method   103
       Data Collection Methods   105
       Selecting the Optimal Data
         Collection Method   113
       Sample Size Determination   113
       Summary   118

   7. STATISTICAL ANALYSIS   121

       Introduction   121
       Continuous versus Categorical Data ...   122
       Measurement Scales   126
       Descriptive Statistics   128

Chapter		Page
	Inferential Statistics	132
	Parametric Statistical Tests	134
	Non-Parametric Statistical Tests	135
	Selecting the Proper Statistical Method	135
	Common Parametric Statistical Techniques	136
	Common Non-Parametric Statistics	144
	Null Hypotheses, Statistical Significance, and Alpha Levels	145
	Lying with Statistics	148
	Summary	149
8.	PRACTICAL COMPUTER USE	155
	Introduction	155
	Computer Compatibility of Instruments and Data Input Methods	155
	Data Input and Storage Methods	160
	Data Dictionary	165
	Suggested Computer Programs with Examples	166
	What Happens Inside the Computer?	178
	Analyzing Computer Print-Outs	179
	Summary	180
9.	WRITING THE FINAL REPORT	187
	Introduction	187
	The Optimum Doctoral/Professional Research Report	188
	Writing Style—APA or Turabian?	199
	Graphic Technique Recommendations	215
	Eight Critical Guidelines in Dissertation or Professional Research Writing	224
	Summary	225
10.	THE FINAL REPORT PRESENTATION	231
	Introduction	231
	Before the Final Presentation	231
	During the Final Presentation	232
	Summary	232
INDEX	....	241

List of Tables

		Page
1.1	Pro/Con Preliminary Idea Worksheet	4
1.2	Time Estimate Example	10
2.1	Thesaurus Keywords (ERIC System)	17
2.2	Subject Index (ERIC System)	20
2.3	Author Index (ERIC System)	21
2.4	Document Resumes (ERIC System)	22
2.5	Summary of Reference System Structure ..	24
2.6	The Literature Review Index Card System	27
3.1	Null, Research, and Alternate Hypotheses	36
4.1	Cost Estimates—Example	48
5.1	A Clockwork Example—Validity and Reliability	54
5.2	Forms of Instrument Validity	56
5.3	Reasonable Validity Coefficients Ranges for Criterion-Related Validity Measures	59
5.4	Instrument Validity Summary	61
5.5	Instrument Reliability Summary	65
5.6	Reasonable Reliability Coefficient Ranges	67
5.7	LERTAP Item Analysis	68
5.8	Published Instrument Source Books	74
5.9	Instrument Evaluation Chart, Example	80
5.10	Likert-Type Response Widths	86
5.11	Evaluation of Likert-Type Response Widths	87
5.12	Pilot Test Evaluation—Example	92
6.1	Choosing the Optimal Sampling Technique	106
6.2	Sampling Method Hierarchy	109
6.3	Choosing the Optimal Data Collection Method	114

6.4   Sample Size Adjustments   116
6.5   Sample Size Adjustments, Example   117

7.1   Continuous and Categorical Data   124
7.2   Measurement Scales   127
7.3   Types and Uses of Descriptive
        Statistics (Commonly used with
        Interval or Ratio Measurement
        Scales)   129
7.4   Calculation Examples of Common
        Descriptive Statistics   133
7.5   Selection Guide for Common Statistical
        Methods   137
7.6   Selecting the Appropriate Statistical
        Test: For Difference (2 or more
        Groups)   138
7.7   Selecting the Appropriate Statistical
        Test: For Relationships
        (1 group)   139

8.1   Computer-Compatible Instrument,
        Simplified Example   158
8.2   Coding Form using Data Responses
        from Table 8.1   159
8.3   Computer Card Diagram using Table
        8.2 Coding Form   161
8.4   Multiple Cards (Records) per
        Respondent   162
8.5   Coding Form using Data Responses from
        Table 8.4   163
8.6   Computer Compatible Instrument for use
        with the Data Dictionary, Example
        Following   168
8.7   The Data Dictionary   172
8.8   SPSS Sample Program   177
8.9   The Computer Process Illustrated   181
8.10   Summary Table of Pearson's
        Correlations   182
8.11   Summary Table of Two-Way Chi-Square
        Tests   183

9.1   The Optimum Dissertation/Professional
        Research Report Outline   188
9.2   Graphic Technique for Frequency
        Distributions   216

9.3   Graphic Technique for Descriptive
        Statistics Reporting   217
9.4   Graphic Techniques for t-Test
        Reporting, Example 1 of 4   219
                 Example 2 of 4   220
                 Example 3 of 4   221
                 Example 4 of 4   222
9.5   Graphic Technique for ANOVA Reporting .. 223
9.6   Graphic Technique for Chi-Square
        Test Reporting   226
9.7   Techniques for Personal Interview
        Reporting (Non-Statistical),
        Style 1 of 2   227
                 Style 2 of 2   228

10.1   The 15 Doctoral Morals Revisited 236

List of Worksheets

		Page
1.1	Pro/Con Preliminary Idea Worksheet	5
1.2	Time Estimate	11
2.6	Master Card Templates	28
3.1A	Developing Null, Research, and Alternate Hypotheses	37
3.1B	Answers	38
4.1	Cost Estimates	49
5.9	Instrument Evaluation Chart	82
5.12	Pilot Test Evaluation	94
6.1A	Choosing the Optimal Sampling Technique	107
6.1B	Choosing the Optimal Sampling Technique	108
8.7	The Data Dictionary	173
9.1	Research Report Outline	200
10.1	Oral Presentation Outline—15 Minutes of Opening Remarks	234

Introduction

OVERVIEW

Why a practical guidebook for doctoral dissertations or professional research? In years of graduate level teaching, private consulting and group seminar instruction regarding dissertation production, statistical analysis, and research design, the need for this type of guidebook and course textbook became more obvious.

Throughout past dissertation seminars, the author noticed that the majority of graduate students had excellent (or at least adequate) coursework behind them. Further, most doctoral students were quite serious about upgrading their professional credentials and career aspirations. Overall, doctoral students genuinely wanted to produce a high quality dissertation; but something seemed lacking. It wasn't the student's ability, interest, or motivation . . . what was it? "Production skill" was that elusive missing ingredient.

Can a guidebook such as this really work? Yes! This document, truly the only one of its kind, will detail, in a clear, concise, and practical format, how to gather all of one's past graduate and undergraduate knowledge, synthesize it, add new skills, and come out not only surviving, but with a totally professional research document. Thus, "production skill," that missing ingredient, has been finally eliminated. It is the author's sincere intent to provide students with a simple, yet practical guide to the production of quality dissertations or other professional research documents.

FORMAT OF THE GUIDEBOOK

This guidebook, being unique in its approach, requires a brief explanation of its format. First, throughout the book's narrative text, numbered points in list form are frequently provided. These lists should always be reviewed in the order in which they are presented. Numerous tables are also found for clarification purposes and often, correspondingly numbered worksheets are provided for the reader's personal use.

Checklists appear at the end of each chapter, and the reader is encouraged to complete such checklists thoroughly. Lastly, each chapter concludes with an extremely valuable element; a listing of references and suggested readings. Only documents of high practical worth to doctoral or professional researchers are included here. The reference lists have been compiled only after a painstaking review of available volumes. Appropriate use of the reading list should save the researcher countless hours wandering about in the library, trying to find the "right" books.

It is realized, of course, that not all researchers may need the entire contents of this comprehensive guidebook; the chapters are designed independently for that reason. The reader should feel free to turn directly to the specific chapters of need. The overall purpose of this document is to provide a truly innovative and practical guide to students.

RESEARCH PROPOSALS AND
THE USE OF THE GUIDEBOOK

First, research proposals are generally in an established writing format, particular to each university or organization. The proposal should always include a brief overview of the study's need and intent, research and null hypotheses, instruments, sampling, and statistical analysis anticipated. Parts of each of these sections can be used again in the final report. Most notably, the discussion of the study's need and intent in the proposal should serve as the foundation in Chapter I of the final report, which needs to "sell" the research topic.

Note that the material presented in each chapter of this guidebook is directly applicable to the topics covered in proposals as well.

Developing Research Ideas

INTRODUCTION

Where does a researcher start? How does one arrive at a feasible research topic? Three channels exist for developing preliminary ideas:

1 Replication
2 Advisor Recommendation
3 Original Idea

Each method will be discussed, in order, below:

1 One way to get a preliminary idea is the replication approach. In hopes of clearing up some confusion, a replication does not mean taking someone's earlier study and redesigning it one's own way. Further, a replication does not necessarily involve previously collected (i.e., secondary) data. A replication, in its true form, involves finding a research study and repeating it in exactly the same way. As one may imagine, replication studies have numerous "pros" and "cons" attached to them. A significant "pro" is in the fact that one decision can be made (to replicate) and the rest of the research design and analysis decisions are generally made as well.

Why else replicate? Perhaps it is decided to repeat a study done a few years ago because it was interesting at the time, and now a re-test of the previous conclusions is desired. Replication is convenient in the fact that all the design questions and various statistical parameter issues are already decided upon. The researcher simply collects new data and compares new findings to the old results.

Is replication an academically worthy method? Indeed! It is quite simply the precise basis of all science. It is only by replication that Truth has ever been approached and subsequently defined.

How can one find a study to replicate? Start by reviewing literature. Select a broad subject matter area of interest, then utilize various search mechanisms

1

for literature review (presented in Chapter II). Next, decide on a specific study, obtain a copy of the work, and design the new research identically to it. Lastly, collect, analyze, and compare findings and conclusions to that previous work. Some advisors don't like replication studies; they want students to do "original" research or an idea of the advisor's own choosing. Sometimes, original studies result in "re-inventing the wheel." Use caution.

2   A second way to get a preliminary idea is directly from one's advisor—a very common approach with some intrinsic plus factors. Perhaps, for whatever reason, the advisor recommends doing a study on a particular topic. Obviously, if one designs and completes the research in a way in which the advisor suggested originally, there will be little remaining to be scrutinized by committee members. In this case, one can, and should, popularize the fact that the project was the advisor's suggestion. However, ensure that you sincerely like the advisor-suggested topic in the first place! Remember that, in the final analysis, the research will be attributed only to you.

3   The final and most common method of getting a preliminary idea involves the development of an original project. As already mentioned, that's easier to say than it is to do. Original ideas can be generated in a number of ways. Start with a very general interest and begin doing literature reviews by computer and by hand (more about literature searches in Chapter II).

As an alternative, one may start a literature review with a replication idea in mind. Later, it may be found that a study to be replicated doesn't measure up exactly to how it sounded when you first read about it in its summary form. Nonetheless, it is possible that in reading the full study, a totally original idea may be derived. It is common to end up with an original idea derived from the search for a replication study.

Problem: What if you're at a complete and total zero point and have no preliminary research ideas whatever?

Solution: Stop everything for a week or two. You are overpressuring yourself! Getting preliminary project ideas just simply isn't that hard.

Eventually you will get an idea; perhaps (and hopefully) multiple ideas. Consider developing three to five ideas by any of the three methods just described. Before meeting with the advisor, it is strongly suggested that three to five preliminary ideas be available for discussion.

Lastly, don't fall into a trap by thinking that these preliminary ideas, at such an early stage, have to be exactly conceptualized. Don't get too specific too fast; it could create disaster later.

DEVELOPING A FINAL WORKABLE IDEA

How should each of your preliminary ideas be ana- lyzed for their feasibility? The Pro/Con Preliminary Idea Sheet provides an accurate method to assess this question (see Table 1.1).

Taking each preliminary idea, one at a time, write out every possible element that would make this idea a good one or a bad one to study. This Worksheet (1.1) is not something to be completed in one afternoon. The procedure represents a very critical first step. Don't rush through this process! Researchers are usually anxious to get the data, and start writing chapters. Please wait! Properly completing the Worksheet(s) will save much aggravation in the future. Two to three weeks of thought into the development of these Worksheet(s) is about average.

More specifically, what are the important consid- erations in developing this table? There are five points to seriously consider:

1   When filling in the Pro/Con Preliminary Idea Sheet,
        first and foremost, be honest about it. Ensure
that every consideration gets into the table.

2   Try to make the pros and cons as specific as
        possible. A "pro" might be: "Well, I think I
could get this report published in a couple of journals
if I did it . . ." but more specifically, exactly where
would you intend to publish an article about this?
Exactly how do you feel it would benefit you?

TABLE 1.1

PRO/CON PRELIMINARY IDEA WORKSHEET

Idea	Pro's	Con's
1	*would advance me professionally *very interested in topic *respondents are readily available	*sample too large *hard to generalize results *advisor doesn't like idea *costly *time-consuming
2	*low cost *could be done in 6 weeks *data already available	*not that interested in the topic *clerical support very important for success *no survey work needed, and I would like to
3	*advisor likes the idea *interesting topic to study *already have about half the references	*costly *time-consuming *don't like data collected in the classroom
4		
5		

4

WORKSHEET 1.1

PRO/CON PRELIMINARY IDEA WORKSHEET

Idea   Pro's   Con's

1

- -

2

WORKSHEET 1.1 (continued)

Idea	Pro's	Con's
3		
4		
5		

3   After each table is in a useful and specific form, openly take it to your academic peers, advisors and committee members. Also, try talking with professors or instructors who are not associated with your school, department, or committee. This can sometimes offer great benefits to you in terms of objective suggestions.

4   You will begin to gain respect from the advisor or others by having the pro/con sheet(s) fully developed. They will acknowledge and respect your early efforts and commonly conclude that, "This student is more of a self-starter; they are giving this project a lot of thought; this student isn't just walking in and saying 'please help me!'" The student who comes in with multiple ideas (and multiple pro/con sheets) has also shown some flexibility. Even at this early stage, the researcher has demonstrated some very important qualities: self-motivation, professionalism, and academic interest.

Unfortunately, if you talk to fellow students about whether they have developed a pro/con sheet of preliminary ideas, they probably will wonder what planet you're from! Too many students generally go to their advisor with one idea, or often no ideas! Obviously, the experienced advisor is going to detect this vagueness and not appreciate it.

Although some advisors might dictate, "Do it this way, period," the vast majority of advisors will work with students if these students gain the advisor's respect first (perhaps by using the pro/con sheet). As students present a number of project ideas, the advisor sees that much work has already been put into the process, and it may be surprising to find how many research ideas advisors are actually going to accept, given this situation. Advisors are simply not accustomed to seeing strong preparedness from a doctoral student—but you're going to be different!

After a number of preliminary ideas have been put through the Pro/Con Preliminary Idea Sheet(s) and academic discussions, certain concepts should be naturally emerging as being the most workable. Take only these emerging ideas and consider them against the following specific Four-Point "Final Topic" Test:

1   A topic might sound good, but be impossible to
     handle. If unsure about how to answer this possi-
bility, find out before the signing of the research
proposal.

     For example, consider a survey of all the junior
high schools in a medium-sized city. That sounds relatively easy, doesn't it? Just try conducting a survey
of all the junior high schools in such a community, or
even a sampling of them! What about the possible political ramifications of doing that type of study? What
about administrative "red tape?" What about questionnaire return rates from many different schools in various
locations? Next, consider mailing, return mailing,
follow-up mailing, follow-up telephone calls, etc.
Research logistics and problems can get incredible after
a while, so it is imperative that your true capabilities
are well thought out, even at this very early stage.

2   Your capabilities aside, are you going to have the
     time available to do everything the research will
require? Apply the 150% time rule.

     If the research is estimated to take 1000 hours,
it's probably going to take 1500 hours. It is far better
to know this now as opposed to finding it out later. See
Table 1.2 for a time estimate example, complete with
common research considerations. Worksheet 1.2 is to be
later completed for your actual project. At the bottom
of the Worksheet will be a time total. Multiply that
total by 1.5 and that is probably the final time invest-
ment. It is important to be as accurate as possible in
the original time estimates. Don't think about the 1.5
multiplication factor when estimating the original times.
If unsure, be liberal with the time allotments.

3   Consider if there is some realistic potential for
     this topic in terms of its subsequent publication.
Will the final document help you further your professional career? This is an important consideration to make
at this early point. The final report can be of tremendous value later for professional growth, although it may
not be felt that this is an important consideration at
the moment.

4   Finally, a common attitude among students is,
     "Forget all this; all I want to do is . . .

A. get through this ordeal,
B. get the dissertation signed, and
C. be through with school."

Believe it or not, one may not feel this way when the dissertation is finally complete and represents a respectable volume of professional work. Being truly satisfied with one's hard work can become critically important, and this includes both academic and professional personal satisfaction. If there are some serious concerns about a particular research idea in terms of academic or professional interest in the topic, this early stage is the best point at which to re-evaluate the potential study. The research effort will easily become dry, complex and even boring at times. Select a final workable idea that will be at least reasonably enjoyable.

```
DOCTORAL MORAL I

After a few thousand hours of investment, a
researcher deserves to have a satisfying final
                    product.
```

SUMMARY

After a discussion with your advisor, and a complete review of this chapter, the one best final workable idea should finally emerge. Practice explaining your proposed research effort to friends and peers. Complete Checklist I to ensure a good procedural understanding of the idea development process before continuing into the next chapter.

TABLE 1.2

TIME ESTIMATE EXAMPLE

Activity	Example Time Estimate (in hours)
I. Developing a Dissertation Idea	30
II. Literature Review	80
III. Methods and Procedures	20
IV. Statistical Analysis	30
V. Interpret Results	70
VI. Write Final Document	120
Total Time Estimate	350

Apply "150% Rule" (__350__ x 1.50 = __525__)

TOTAL TIME EXPECTED = __525__ hours

WORKSHEET 1.2

TIME ESTIMATE

Activity	Time Estimate (in hours)
I. Developing a Dissertation Idea	
II. Literature Review	
III. Methods and Procedures	
IV. Statistical Analysis	
V. Interpret Results	
VI. Write Final Document	
Total Time Estimate	

Apply "150% Rule" (_____ X 1.50 = _____)

TOTAL TIME EXPECTED = _____

REFERENCES AND SUGGESTED READINGS

The list below has been selected with the utmost care. The listing has been purposely limited to only those texts which are of a great practical and useful value to most doctoral or professional researchers. Not every entry may be still in print, but generally a search to locate such a book will be very worthwhile. Entries denoted with a double asterisk (**) are those highly recommended for the topic specified. Parenthetical comments for each entry are added by this author.

Best, J. Research in Education, 3rd ed. Englewood Cliffs: Prentice-Hall, 1977.

    (Some good ideas and pointers; see pp. 18-34 particularly.)

Fox, D. J. The Research Process in Education. New York: Holt, Rinehart and Winston, Inc., 1969.

    (A good general purpose text.)

Hyman, H. Secondary Analysis of Sample Surveys. New John Wiley, 1972.

    (Interesting methods for research using data already collected for purposes of a different study.)

**Kerlinger, F. N. Foundations of Behavioral Research, 2nd ed. New York: Holt, Rinehart and Winston, Inc., 1973.

    (An excellent text in this area; see particularly Chapter 1, pp. 2-16, and Chapter 17, pp. 300-314.)

CHECKLIST I

( ) 1. Do you understand the advantages and disadvantages of: Replication, advisor recommendation and original ideas in the context of developing preliminary research ideas?

( ) 2. Develop three to five preliminary ideas. Consider replication, advisor recommendation and original ideas.

( ) 3. Do not overly try to get the preliminary idea(s) too specific at this early stage.

( ) 4. Honestly complete the Pro/Con Idea Sheet (Worksheet 1.1), creating one such table for each preliminary idea. This could take two to three weeks or more.

( ) 5. Meet with advisor, etc. and discuss each preliminary idea. Display the pro/con tables devised.

( ) 6. Eventually witness the emergence of one (or two) final research topics.

( ) 7. Test the potential final research topic against the four-point Final Topic Test. Re-work the topic as necessary until it passes this topic test.

( ) 8. Review suggested readings and comments.

( ) 9. The final research topic should be firmly decided at this point. It is a clear and concise topic which can be explained to an appropriate audience. Explain the topic to a friend or academic peer just as a test.

ERIC Volumes

Microfiche Reader/Copier

Literature Reviews

INTRODUCTION

After developing the final research topic, it is time to begin a more in-depth review of references. There is much confusion about conducting this element of the research process. The presentation will describe a number of procedures regarding this often cumbersome work, with common literature review sources and digging techniques explained.

THE PURPOSE OF A LITERATURE REVIEW

A literature review is meant primarily to set the foundation for the study's hypotheses. The literature review allows a reader to better understand the research problem in terms of historical background, theoretical framework, and current research developments or trends. It is critically important that the literature review includes only the most relevant articles. When done correctly, within logical and reasonable criteria, the literature review can add excellent dimensions to the final document.

What sources are readily available for a literature review? In what order should one try to organize the search? Both of these questions are crucial and are addressed in the upcoming sections.

JOURNAL TITLES

As the first step, obtain titles of journals pertinent to the research topic. The professional journal market is overwhelming in its size. No one is aware of every journal that is relevant to any one field of interest. Consult directories directly at the university library or see the text by Best (1977) listed in the References and Suggested Readings list at this chapter's conclusion. Review journal listings carefully and list all the entries that are even remotely relevant to your research topic. Depending upon the specific research topic, the journal listings search could be a time-consuming process, but nonetheless an important one. The journal list will become very helpful when completing the computerized literature search to be done later.

SEARCHING IN ERIC, PSYCHOLOGICAL
ABSTRACTS, AND RELATED DOCUMENT
FILE SYSTEMS

After acquiring the listing of relevant journal titles, proceed to a review of computer generated references. This review will involve such systems as ERIC (Educational Resource Index Center), Sociological Abstracts, Psychological Abstracts, and many others. Using the help of a qualified and experienced reference librarian, many references can be quickly located, based on specific subject heading(s). Using computer searches is an excellent methodology, and the process itself requires a further description, together with explanatory tables.

When using ERIC (or a similar computerized reference system) one finds a very sophisticated research tool. These reference files are massive "card catalogs" consisting of research documents and articles that have been published or presented throughout the world. The libraries which house these reference systems either have or may order copies of the documents referenced.

How does a researcher conduct a computer or hand search of these huge reference files? Using a series of tables, the procedure is demonstrated by utilizing a practical example from ERIC. The method is the same for use with other search systems (e.g., Psychological Abstracts, Sociological Abstracts). Simply follow the 12-Step Literature Review Process:

1   Table 2.1 (extracted from the ERIC Thesaurus Guide) indicates major headings in bold print. Suppose the research topic concerns parent-child relationships. Initially, examine the ERIC Thesaurus looking for major headings (bold print) relating to this research topic. Under the major heading "Parents" (obviously a related term to the topic), the sub-heading "Parent-Child Relationship" is then located. In virtually any research endeavor, a Thesaurus heading or sub-heading will either exactly or closely fit the research topic. Remember to review all Thesaurus indexes related to the field of interest.

16

TABLE 2.1

THESAURUS KEYWORDS (ERIC SYSTEM)

unseling
Counseling
tudes
ld Relationship
rticipation
hool Relationship
Teacher Confer-

Teacher Coopera-

ATION   Jul. 1966
81   RIE: 679
Education
tal Background
ts
t Workshops

ns

NT CONFERENCES

D EDUCATION
               Jul. 1973
2   RIE: 50
is designed to help
boys and girls pre-
r effective parent-
y learning about
evelopment and the
parents, and by
g closely with young
n
Life Education
Development
Rearing
ily Life
ily Relationship
ent Child Relationship
ent Role

INFLUENCE   Jul. 1966
JE: 288   RIE: 302
nily Influence
hers
hers
ent Role
nts

Parent
Parents
Teacher Responsibility

PARENT ROLE   Jul. 1966
    CIJE: 517   RIE: 525
UF Father Role #
    Mother Role #
RT Family Role
    Fathers
    Mothers
    Parenthood Education
    Parent Influence
    Parents
    Student Role

PARENTS   Jul. 1966
    CIJE: 205   RIE: 270
NT Catholic Parents
    Fathers
    Grandparents
    Lower Class Parents
    Middle Class Parents
    Mothers
    Working Parents
BT Groups
RT Family (Sociological Unit)
    Family Life
    Family Problems
    Heads Of Households
    Home Visits
    One Parent Family
    Parental Aspiration
    Parental Background
    Parent Associations
    Parent Attitudes
    Parent Child Relationship
    Parent Conferences
    Parent Education
    Parent Influence
    Parent Participation
    Parent Reaction
    Parent Responsibility
    Parent Role
    Parent School Relati

rent Rel
ramily Relationship
RT Emancipated Stude
    Family School Rela
    Parent Child Relatic
    Parents
    Parent Student Conf
    School Phobia
    Students

Parent Study Group
USE PARENT CONFERENC

PARENT TEACHER CONFEREN
              Ju
    CIJE: 68   RIE:
UF Teacher Parent
    ences
BT Conferences
RT Faculty Workload
    Parent Counseling
    Parents
    Parent School Rela
    Parent Teacher
    tion
    Teachers

PARENT TEACHER COOPERA
              Ju
    CIJE: 150   RIE: 1
UF Teacher Parent Co
    tion
RT Cooperative Planning
    Home Visits
    Parent Counseling
    Parent School Relati
    Parent Teacher
    ences

PARENT WORKSHOPS
    CIJE: 33   RIE:
BT Workshops
RT Parent Conferences
    Parent Education
    Parents

Pari

Courtesy: ERIC

2   At the encircled "a" on Table 2.1, the sub-heading "Parent-Child Relationship" is located. This means that this reference system (ERIC in this case), uses this sub-heading phrase as a keyword for its article categorization. This sub-heading can now be utilized, both by computer search and hand search methodologies. Most times many keywords will be used together to further focus the search.

3   Occasionally a researcher may run into problems in defining of keywords. In this instance, consult a reference librarian who has experience with the ERIC (or other) reference system.

4   Conduct the computer search with the librarian, using the keyword phrases. The computer will provide a listing of the articles, together with an abstract and procurement information.

5   After reviewing the computer search print-out, purchase copies of the articles that come closest to the research topic. If not sure about a particular article's relevance, it is best to obtain the article.

6   Note the latest date on the computer search print-out. Then by hand, still using the identical keywords, use the reference system's subject indexes to get back up to the current date. This is a critically important step!

7   Remember that listing of journal titles made earlier? Ensure that those titles are all within the computer search system(s) just used. If not, a review by hand of these periodicals is mandatory.

In conducting a hand search, refer to the reference system's Subject Index (large, bound volumes), and go back to just before the latest date shown on the computer print-out. Use the identical computer search keyword(s) as done previously and skim the article titles. Copy down identification numbers of articles that might relate to the research topic. Repeat the procedure for all keywords up to the current date. (Use this procedure for Steps 6-7.)

In an example, the tracing of one article under "Parent-Child Relationship" is now demonstrated. The article is titled, "Changes in the Adolescent-Parent Relationship According to Sex Role." The article identification number is noted as "ED-144-907." This number allows the researcher to easily get more information on this specific article (see Table 2.2).

8 Suppose that from another computer search or other academic source, the researcher is already aware of respected authors in the field of interest. In this case, simply refer to the Author Index of the reference search system for any one particular time interval and find the author's name and article titles presented or published during that time period. In this continuing example, Table 2.3 indicates the same article now listed under the author's name (see letter "a" highlighted in the table). Again, of course, the identical article reference number appears (ED-144-907).

9 Table 2.4 is a sample page of the Document Resume. Find the article identification number, obtained from either the subject or author index. The example article, ED-144-907, is quickly located. Also, it is discovered here that the same article is in Sociological Abstracts as number SO 010377. Further, the author, the title, the date it was published, and a note showing in what form the article was presented, is shown.

Specifically, this article was a 16-page paper which was presented at the annual meeting of the Western Social Sciences Association in Denver, Colorado on April 21-25, 1977. The article will cost $1.67 in hard copy ("HC"), meaning on paper stock. "MF" refers to a document cost of 83¢ in microfilm/fiche form. The university library may have the microfilm/fiche of the entire 16-page paper and, if the library also has a microfilm/ fiche reader/copier, it is possible to copy the article immediately. If the above-mentioned equipment is unavailable, send for the article through the library system. Return time should be one to three weeks.

10 Returning again to the Document Resume (Table 2.4), of additional importance are the other descriptors shown, such as "Adolescence," "Comparative Analysis," "Elementary/Secondary Education," etc. These are all other keywords which also could have located this same article. Optionally, return into the

TABLE 2.2

SUBJECT INDEX

(ERIC SYSTEM)

Subject Index

rban School System and Their Relationships
Conflict in Goal Orientation and Achieve-
nt.
ED 144 216//

Study of Thirteen Catholic High Schools in
ater Cincinnati.
ED 144 186

t Awareness Measure
er Doesn't Know Best: Parents' Awareness
heir Children's Linguistic, Cognitive, and
ctive Development.
ED 144 713

t Child Relationship
Abusive Environment and the Child's
aptation.
ED 149 222

tachment Behaviors in Abused Children Dur-
g Brief Separation from Mother.
ED 148 082

On Becoming a "Modern Parent" in the
1920's.
ED 148 468

Benefits to Adolescents of Informal Helping
Relationships with Their Parents and Peers.
ED 147 665

Between Grownups & Kids: Conference
Proceedings (Austin, Texas, August 27, 1977).
ED 149 519

Changes in the Adolescent-Parent Relationship
according to Sex Role.
ED 144 907

A Comparison of Infant Interaction with Stran-
gers and Parents.
ED 148 458

Descriptive Study of the Status and Change
Attitudes and Child Development
wledge of the Preschool Parents Involved
School/Home Program.
ED 145 963

Double Bind Theory of Communication as
tes to Communication Apprehension and
ted Personality Development.
ED 143 039//

g Among Rural Youth with Implications
l Institutional Development.
ED 144 729

Parenting in Contemporary America:
lutions and S

Proce...   ...ruel nor
...   ...united States Supre
Court's Decision in "Ingraham v. Wright."
ED 145 5

Pointers for Parents, 1974.
ED 146 2

Pronouns and the Social Self in Mother-Chi
Conversation.
ED 145 96

Q's & A's on Child Mental Health: An Inte
view with Dr. Berry Brazelton.
ED 143 17

The Relationship Between Black Father-Chi
Interactions and Self-Esteem in Preschool Chi
dren.
ED 148 942

Relationships Among Children's Perceptions o
Parent Behavior, Parents' Inferences of Their
Children's Perceptions, and Parents' Self-Per
ceptions.
ED 145 306

Separation and Divorce: Annotated Bibliog-
raphy of Selected Literature for Children and
Teens. Also, Recommended Reading for
Parents.
ED 143 901

Sex Differences in Verbal Interaction Patterns
of Mothers and Their Preschool Children.
ED 146 518

Situational Determinants of Parental Behavior.
Effects of Competing Cognitive Activity.
ED 149 251

Stress Affects Maternal Punitiveness: A Model
for Investigating Child Abuse.
ED 149 530

The Structure of Infant-Adult Social
Reciprocity. A Cross Cultural Study of Face to
Face Interaction: Gusii Infants and Mothers.
ED 144 701

Talking about the There and Then.
ED 144 39

Theme: Parents and Reading.
ED 145 3

Training Parents as Home Teachers: A Revi
of Research.
ED 147 (

Violence Towards Children in the Un
States.
ED 143

Men as Fathers of Adolescents.
ED 14

Courtesy: ERIC

20

TABLE 2.3

AUTHOR INDEX

(ERIC SYSTEM)

ce.

ED 148 399

tream Migration: Are
t a Disadvantage?

ED 149 950

ıu

and Negative Audience
' Nonverbal Performance
ir Attitudes.

ED 143 049//

ocesses of Unskilled Writers
el.

ED 147 819

Staff: Who Cares for the Care

ED 149 197

æl

x and Relationship on Self-Disclo-

ED 145 326//

ıne Szutu
ation and Evaluation of Sponsored
ial Learning. CAEL Institutional Re-
3. University of California at Los An-
vised Edition.

ED 148 858

ohn
Study of Success, Attrition and Follow-
ıds Junior College Entering Freshman
Fall 1971.

ED 149 811

Case Study of Writing.

ED 149 375

Mode on Written Syntactic
IV--Across-The-Grades' Dif-
ral Summary. Report No. 30.

ED 147 831

Process   for   Class-
ation   anª

used Curriculum
Learning. Some Ramifications f
Education in the 1980s.

The Effects of the Social Science
on Education Decision Makers: A
Perspective Research Report.

A Process for Comprehensive
Change: The Experimental Schools
Rural America - A Case Study (197.

Peters, Richard O., Ed.
Man in His World.

ED

Petersen, Evelyn Ann
A Descriptive Study of the Status and C
in   Attitudes   and   Child   Develop
Knowledge of the Preschool Parents Invo
in a School/Home Program.

ED 145 9

Petersen, Nancy
An Investigation of Item Obsolescence in the
Scholastic Aptitude Test.

ED 148 862

Peterson, Donald C.
Milestone 25 (NIU's Outdoor Teacher Education Programs -- Twenty-five Years of Pioneer-
ing). Lorado Taft Field Campus Commemora-
tive Brochure.

ED 148 514

Peterson, Eric E.
The Communication Model Perspective of Oral
Interpretation.

ED 143 055

Peterson, Evan T.
Changes in the Adolescent-Parent Relationship
according to Sex Role.

ED 144 907

Peterson, Gary W.
Attainment   Rather   Than   Competence: A
Legitimate Basis for the Certification of Learn-
ing Outcomes.

ED 145 76ſ
Curriculum of Attainments. Final Report.

ED 148 ˉ

Peterson, Jim
vey of Children's Interests in Gr
ь Bulletin No 1

Courtesy: ERIC

TABLE 2.4

DOCUMENT RESUMES

(ERIC SYSTEM)

evidence on the relationship between work related technology and job satisfaction. A review of
research dealing with social crisis and disaster is
presented in the next article. The third paper
views measurement in social stratification.
...nd studies which use a survey sample and cen-
...data, an overview of family interaction litera-
..., and methods for modeling the structure of
...ationships among variables with systems of
...uations are treated in the next three papers.
...e seventh article examines mortality trends.
...e eighth looks at the social structure of Main-
...nd China. Surveys of the current state of the
...ield of political socialization, of empirical and
theoretical investigations conducted by symbolic
interactionists, and of research in the areas of socialization and personality are presented. The last
four papers deal with mobility and stratification
in Russia, recent trends in Polish sociology,
demography and the family, and the study of
slavery. (Author/RM)

ED 144 907   SO 010 377
Peterson, Evan T.
**Changes in the Adolescent-Parent Relationship ac-
cording to Sex Role.**
Pub Date Apr 77
Note—16p.; Paper presented at Annual Meeting
of the Western Social Science Association
(Denver, Colorado, April 21-25, 1977)
EDRS Price MF-$0.83 HC-$1.67 Plus Postage.
Descriptors—*Adolescents, *Changing Attitudes,
Comparative Analysis, Elementary Secondary
Education, Fathers, Mothers, Parent Attitudes,
*Parent Child Relationship, Parent Influence,
*Parent Role, Sex Role, *Social Change, Social
Science Research
The study examined changes that have taken
place between 1968 and 1976 in terms of
adolescent-parent relationships as defined by the
interest in and control over adolescents by
parents. Also, a comparison was made of the different ways in which young girls and boys are so-
cialized. Questionnaire responses from 7,810
adolescents in 46 high schools collected in 1968
were compared with responses from 7,508
adolescents in 52 schools in 1976. All major re-
gions of the country were represented. The
questionnaires contained scales of paternal control, maternal control, paternal interest, and
maternal interest. Control referred to parental attempts to modify children's behavior in ac-
cordance with predetermined standards of conduct. Interest referred to degree of parental concern for their children. Results showed an increase in both interest and control in 1976. Consistently, the mother was seen to display greater
interest and control than the father, regardless of
the child's sex. In 1976, there was a greater difference in parents' levels of interest and control
over boys as opposed to girls than there was in
1968. This may be due to parental concern about
recent developments such as sexual permissive-
ness and the drug subculture. (Author/AV)

...ey agree" i
...o statements al
... ...nalysis of responses indicates
young adults as represented by the sample
ambivalent toward childlessness. Students
were younger and more religious tended to l
negative attitudes toward childlessness. Stud
with positive attitudes tended to value
freedom and were less religious and jea
(AV)

ED 144 909   SO 01C
Armstrong, William L.   And Others
**Educational and Occupational Aspirations a
pectations of Black and White College Stu**
Pub Date 77
Note—13p.; Paper presented at Annual N
of the Southwestern Sociological Ass
(Dallas, Texas, March 30-April 2, 1977)
EDRS Price MF-$0.83 HC-$1.67 Plus Post
Descriptors—Black Students, Caucasian S
*College Students, Comparative A
*Educational Attitudes, Educational So
*Ethnic Groups, *Expectation, Higher
tion, *Occupational Aspiration, Predict
ables, Racial Factors
The paper compares educational and o
tional aspirations and expectations of 50(
and white students from a San Antonio c
Previous research had produced conflicting
ries of social class and race as determina
expectations. This study employed a se
ministered questionnaire which included the
cupational Aspiration Scale (OAS). The
provided to every respondent the same set of
cupational alternatives in terms of ideali
aspirations and realistic expectations. Ot
questions assessed educational aspirations and
pectations, as well as independent variab
through which racial and social class differenc
could be identified. Results indicated that blac
and whites had similar educational aspiration
but that blacks had higher realistic expectation
More whites than blacks had low occupation
aspirations. Blacks had higher occupational e
pectations. These results, which conflict wi
some previous research, may be due to sam
bias and the effects of recent legislation to
prove educational and occupational opportuni
for minority groups. The results support
theory that race, not social class, influence
pectations and aspirations. (AV)

ED 144 910   95   SO 01C
Azzouz, Azzedine, Comp.   And Others
**Selected Bibliography of Educational Mat
Maghreb, Algeria, Libya, Morocco, T
Vol. 9, No. 1, 1975 [And] Vol. 9, No. 2, 1**
Agence Tunisienne de Public Relations,
(Tunisia).
Spons Agency—National Science Found
Washington, D.C.; Office of Education
HEW), Washington, D.C.
Pub Date [76]
Note—7°
                             ... hard copy fr
                             ... of origi.

Subject Index (Table 2.2) and refer to these new keywords to possibly find additional articles regarding the research topic.

11   Next in the Document Resume is a short paragraph describing what each study was about. Read this immediately so as to not waste time obtaining the hard copy or the microfiche of an article that is not germane to the research topic. If the article would reasonably seem to fit into the literature review, obtain it.

12   Lastly, at the end of the summary in the Document Resume notice, within parentheses, who wrote the descriptive paragraph.

The previous 12-step procedure covers the methodology of ERIC literature searches quite fully. The procedure within other reference systems is nearly identical. Many articles in Psychological Abstracts, Sociological Abstracts or other similar directories would also be located through the ERIC system. The overlap between the many reference systems is substantial, but review all the systems to be safe. Table 2.5 illustrates the overall structure of the reference systems.

REFERENCE SEARCH WARNINGS

There are a number of warnings that must be included for those using the sophisticated technology of reference searches such as ERIC or Psychological Abstracts computerized reference systems. A few of the points below have been discussed earlier, but certainly their reiteration is justified. Consider the Reference Search Warnings List:

1   Take time reviewing the keywords selected in either hand or computer searches. The difference in one keyword could change the number of articles found in drastic proportions.

2   Utilize an ERIC-experienced reference librarian for assistance in both computer and hand searches.

3   Limit the initial search to an absolute maximum of 50-75 entries. Again, a slight narrowing or broadening of the keywords can easily alter the articles found.

TABLE 2.5

SUMMARY OF REFERENCE SYSTEM STRUCTURE

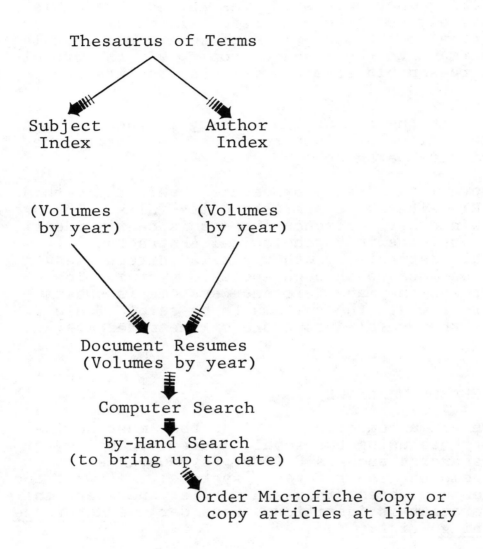

Thesaurus of Terms

Subject
Index

Author
Index

(Volumes
by year)

(Volumes
by year)

Document Resumes
(Volumes by year)

Computer Search

By-Hand Search
(to bring up to date)

Order Microfiche Copy or
copy articles at library

4   Be sure to check the latest date on the computer-
     ized search print-out and do a by-hand review of
     the subject indexes to get up to the current date.
     This is very important!

5   Ensure that the reference systems used have in-
     cluded the journal titles you had initially
     listed. If not, complete a hand search of all the
     excluded journals.

OTHER LITERATURE REVIEW
SOURCES AND SEARCH METHODS

     An excellent source of book titles and summaries
is Buro's Books in Print. Review a current edition of
this reference source to find texts which may pertain to
the research topic.

     Secondly, review Dissertation Abstracts for list-
ings of past doctoral dissertations. This source can
sometimes be cumbersome and frustrating to use, but it
is still worth the effort. Many Dissertation Abstract
documents may overlap into other larger reference files
(e.g., ERIC), but this is, unfortunately, not totally
consistent.

     Finally, there may be some other non-standard,
local resources available to you. Check with your
reference librarian and advisor.

HOW MANY REFERENCES ARE ENOUGH?

     How can one reasonably limit the literature re-
view? How can it be finally decided which references
should go in and which should be left out? These
questions are, by far, the most common relative to a
literature review.

     After examining various articles, texts, and
dissertations from the search efforts, a researcher will
vividly (painfully?) be aware of the volume of documents
available. If the total number of documents is low
relative to normal expectations (usually less than about
thirty articles), then consider methods to increase the
listing. A good technique here is to include more historical articles which will then act as a preface to the
more specific literature review. Further, perhaps the
advisor or committee members have favorite authors which

can be included in a more general way, even if the articles don't exactly fit the research topic.

If burdened with too many references (50 or more), finely focus and reduce the literature review. Include only landmark studies and dispense with the rest. Use only articles which have a direct and specific bearing on the research topic. Reduce <u>historical or theoretical articles</u> to a minimum level (approximately <u>five to ten</u> references).

Remember, the written literature review need not be long to be good. Consider the final selection of reference material carefully, using a procedural system which can be explained (and defended) later. The following section will help organize the references.

THE LITERATURE REVIEW
INDEX CARD SYSTEM

Every literature review requires a good organizational system. Make a 3 x 5 index card for every reference and color code these cards based upon the four sub-categories suggested below. The color coding procedure will help tremendously in consolidating or reducing the reference list later.

For example, in a literature review regarding the topic's historical development, use blue-coded cards for all references. In a further review, perhaps concerning recent research developments, use white-coded cards for these references. See Table 2.6 for more details regarding the use of the Index Card System. Use the example shown in Worksheet 2.6 to make a master card template (two to a sheet), and get numerous copies printed on multi-colored stock before beginning the literature review. Do not skip the Index Card System; it will be of tremendous practical assistance in efficiently completing the literature review segment of the final document.

SUMMARY

Chapter II has described how to conduct a detailed literature review using both computerized and hand search methods. A series of lists and processes were presented for use by the researcher. A suggested reading list is also provided. Checklist II should be completed before continuing to the next chapter.

REFERENCES AND SUGGESTED READINGS

The list below has been selected with the utmost care. The listing has been purposely limited to only those texts which are of a great practical and useful value to most doctoral or professional researchers. Not every entry may be still in print, but generally a search to locate such a book will be very worthwhile. Entries denoted with a double asterisk (**) are those highly recommended for the topic specified. Parenthetical comments for each entry are added by this author.

**Best, J. Research in Education, 3rd ed. Englewood Cliffs: Prentice-Hall, 1977.

(Concerning specifically literature reviews, a very good source book; see pp. 43-85 particularly. Balance of text is good general purpose methods text.)

Fox, D. J. The Research Process in Education. New York: Holt, Rinehart and Winston, Inc., 1969.

(A good general discussion.)

**Tuckerman, B. W. Conducting Educational Research, 2nd ed. New York: Harcourt Brace Jovanovich, Inc., 1978.

(A good literature review source book; see pp. 41-50 particularly. Balance of text is good general information text.)

CHECKLIST II

( ) 1. List all journal titles relevant to the final research topic.

( ) 2. Use the 12-Step Literature Review Process to complete a computer-generated, then hand, literature review.

( ) 3. Review and understand the structure of the literature reference systems (Table 2.5).

( ) 4. Review the Reference Search Warnings List carefully.

( ) 5. Consult other literature reference volumes (i.e., Buro's, Dissertation Abstracts, etc.).

( ) 6. Aim for 30 to 75 references. Try to balance them between the various types of articles (theoretical, historical, current research, past research, and other types).

( ) 7. Utilize the Index Card System (Worksheet 2.6).

( ) 8. Organize the index cards into a logical order for writing. (Much more about writing in Chapter IX of this guidebook.)

( ) 9. Review suggested readings and comments.

Understanding and Developing Hypotheses

INTRODUCTION

hy-poth-e-sis (hi-poth-e-sis) n., pl -ses (-sez).
An assumption subject to verification or proof, as
a conjecture that accounts for a set of facts and
can be used as a basis for further investigation.
[Gk Hypothesis, proposal.]

This chapter will begin by explaining hypothesis
terminology, hopefully once and for all. Hypothesis are
the basic tools of science. While involved in research
enterprises, various strange terminologies regarding
hypotheses present themselves. The confusion usually
starts among these terms:

1   Null Hypothesis
2   Research Hypothesis
3   Alternative Hypothesis
4   Alternate Hypothesis

Even doctoral advisors, committee members, or other
audiences can't always agree on the meaning of the above
terminology! A discussion regarding each of these terms
is well overdue in the field of doctoral or professional
research design.

NULL HYPOTHESIS

The null hypothesis is simply the hypothesis of <u>no
difference</u> or <u>no relationship</u>. This hypothesis is the
strict basis for quantitative science. All inferential
statistical tests that will be used in scientific,
quantitative research are tested against the null hypothesis for statistical significance.

As an example, if studying career education in
high school, a group of students may have received career

education training, while another similar group simply received traditional classroom learning experiences. A null hypothesis might be: "There will be no statistically significant difference in career awareness mean scores between the career education classroom students and the traditional classroom students." Hence, the burden of proof to show a difference in experimental research data always rests with the researcher. There is no difference between the groups, unless statistically demonstrated otherwise.

Thus, the null hypothesis is simply the scientifically stated phrase that can be statistically tested. It usually does not represent what the researcher thinks will be found in the research, but acts strictly as the scientific statement to be tested.

The symbol for the null hypothesis is:

$$H_{(O)n}$$

where "n" is the identification number for any one specific hypothesis. A research project can have a limitless number of null hypotheses, but should always have at least one. Each null hypothesis will need at least one specific statistical test to evaluate the statement. Much more about statistical analysis of null hypotheses in Chapter VII. See examples of null hypotheses in Table 3.1.

RESEARCH HYPOTHESIS

What does the researcher think the study will find? Again, to use the previous example, if studying career education in a high school, one group of students may receive a certain type of career education training, while another group of similar students receives a traditional classroom education. A research hypothesis might then be: "The classroom receiving career education training will score significantly higher on the career education awareness test than will the traditional classroom." By virtue of what one thinks they are going to find, the research hypothesis is so defined. It's that easy.

The symbol for the research hypothesis is:

$$H_{(R)n}$$

where "n" is simply the hypothesis number for identification purposes. A research project can have a limitless number of research hypotheses, but should always have at least one. Important: Each null hypothesis must have a respective research hypothesis. See examples of research hypotheses in Table 3.1.

ALTERNATIVE (OR ALTERNATE) HYPOTHESIS

The alternative or alternate hypothesis is exactly the same thing as the research hypothesis. The symbol for the alternative or alternate hypothesis is:

$$H_{(A)n}$$

with "n" simply acting as an identification number for each alternative hypothesis statement. How did the research, alternative, and alternate hypotheses come to mean the same thing? How did the terms get hopelessly mixed up over the years?

The research hypothesis got its name from the idea that this hypothesis was what one was researching, and hence usually stated what the researcher was hoping to find by the investigation.

In contrast, the alternative or alternate hypothesis came about as a form of scientific terminology, reflecting an "alternative" statement to the null hypothesis. In formal statistical testing, if one rejected the null hypothesis, what was the alternative? The alternative became the "alternative or alternate hypothesis," and, as such, it was so named (see examples of alternative hypotheses in Table 3.1).

Depending upon which text one picks up, the terminology of "research hypothesis," "alternative hypothesis," or "alternate hypothesis" can all be readily found. These terms are all describing the same thing; namely, a hypothesis of difference or relationship, and usually (although not always) these hypotheses are describing what the researcher is hoping to find. Preferably, use the term "research hypothesis" in your work, denoted as:

$$H_{(R)n}$$

DIRECTIONALITY OF RESEARCH HYPOTHESES

Research hypotheses can be either directional (one-tail) or non-directional (two-tail). In a directional research hypothesis, not only is a difference or relationship expected, it is expected in a definite direction. Consider this research hypothesis:

$H_{(R)1}$ Boys will score significantly <u>lower</u> than girls on self-esteem assessment.

Not only is a difference expected, but the direction of the difference is specifically stated. Comparatively, now consider a research hypothesis in which a difference or relationship is expected, but no direction of difference is established:

$H_{(R)2}$ Boys will score significantly different than girls on self-esteem assessment.

$H_{(R)2}$ is quite a different statement than $H_{(R)1}$.

Question: "How does one know if the research hypotheses are to be developed as directional or non-directional?"* This would depend largely on previous results from other studies and the researcher's own instincts. Be sure that the directionality or non-directionality of the research hypotheses can be later defended. (See Table 3.1 for practical examples of both directional and non-directional research hypotheses.) Also remember, the <u>null</u> hypotheses are immune from this entire "directionality" issue, since they are <u>always</u> statements of no difference or no relationship.

After reviewing Table 3.1, try some hypothesis writing. Fill in the blank sections of Worksheet 3.1A; find the answers on Worksheet 3.1B. This is a valuable practice exercise.

DEVELOPING NULL AND RESEARCH HYPOTHESES

<u>There are four critical Hypothesis Development Rules to follow in creating research hypotheses:</u>

34

1   Hypotheses <u>must</u> reflect what the study in essence
        is all about. Ensure that the hypotheses do not
stray from the major issue(s) and thrust of the original
research topic.

2   Hypotheses must be written clearly, without
        ambiguity. Ensure that one hypothesis is <u>only</u>
<u>one</u> hypothesis and is not a compound thought.

3   In the vast majority of cases, the hypotheses in
        a scientific research endeavor must be testable by
quantitative means. Design the study so that appropriate
scores or values are available for quantifying the
information needed relative to testing each null
hypothesis.

4   In most cases, it is best if a statistical test
        assesses <u>one</u> null hypothesis. For example, five
null hypotheses should require five individual statistical tests in most cases.

        Constructing hypotheses which are testable (Point
3, above) is a process which many students want to avoid.
The word "testable" often has chilling side-effects for
some normally very bright and creative people. Believe
it or not, research is generally better and easier if
if the hypotheses are, in fact, measurable. The use of
measurable hypotheses and statistical procedures will
usually make a research project much more credible because there will be established "cut-points" (alpha
levels) at which the findings are either significant or
not significant. The researcher is not open to bias
interpretations and the final report will be a much
easier product to present and, more importantly, to
defend.

        Further, in studies initially appearing to be
descriptive or historical in nature, a testable and
measurable hypothesis can almost always be indirectly
developed. Of course, there will always be a few
occasions when statistical testing will simply not be
feasible or appropriate, but these studies are very rare
and will usually end up as extremely difficult research
endeavors to complete and later defend.

TABLE 3.1

NULL, RESEARCH, AND ALTERNATE HYPOTHESES

NULL HYPOTHESES	RESEARCH (OR ALTERNATE) HYPOTHESES
H(0)1: There will be no statistically significant difference between Republican and Democratic voters in relation to their voting behavior in school millage elections.	H(R)1: There will be a statistically significant difference between Republican and Democratic voters in relation to their voting behavior in school millage elections. (Non-Directional) (2-tail)
H(0)2: There will be no statistically significant difference between adult men and adult women with regard to level of anxiety.	H(R)2: Adult men will have a significantly greater level of anxiety than adult women. (Directional) (1-tail)
H(0)3: There will be no statistically significant correlation (i.e., relationship) between music aptitude and mathematics aptitude among 5th graders in the North County School District.	H(R)3: There will be a significant positive correlation (i.e., relationship) between music aptitude and mathematics aptitude among 5th graders in the North County School District. (Directional) (1-tail)

WORKSHEET 3.1A

DEVELOPING NULL, RESEARCH, AND ALTERNATE HYPOTHESES

NULL HYPOTHESES

RESEARCH (OR ALTERNATE) HYPOTHESES

H(O)1: There is no statistically significant difference between males and females in reading ability.

H(R)1: (Non-Directional) Fill in: _____
_____
_____
_____

H(O)2: Fill in: _____
_____
_____

H(R)2: Children from high income parents will score significantly higher on the math aptitude test than chil- dren from low income parents.

H(O)3: There is no statistically significant correlation (or relationship) between vision ability and coordination among children aged 3 to 5 years.

H(R)3: (Directional) Fill in: _____
_____
_____
_____

Answers on the following page. _____

WORKSHEET 3.1B

ANSWERS

NULL HYPOTHESES

RESEARCH (OR ALTERNATE) HYPOTHESES

H(R)1: (Non-Directional) There will be a statistically significant differ-ence between males and females in reading ability.

H(O)2: There will be no statistically significant difference between children from high income parents or children from low income parents on the math aptitude test.

H(R)3: (Directional) There will be a statistically significant positive correlation between vision ability and coordination among children aged 3 to 5 years.

or

H(R)3: (Directional) There will be a statistically significant negative correlation between vision ability and coordination among children aged 3 to 5 years.

38

> If given a choice, always design measurable and testable hypotheses; it will greatly strengthen the research and reduce potential problems later. Share the research and null hypotheses with your advisor as soon as possible!

REJECTING OR ACCEPTING THE NULL

In a scientific analysis of data, only the null hypothesis is actually "tested" by the statistical procedure applied. In theory, therefore, the null hypothesis is either rejected (i.e., there is a difference or relationship in the data) or the null hypothesis is accepted (i.e., there is no difference or relationship in the data).

THE DOUBLE-WHAMMY SYNDROME AND DIRECTIONAL RESEARCH HYPOTHESES

Sometimes a null hypothesis may be rejected, but the results are, unfortunately, in a contrary direction to that stated by a directional (one-tail) research hypothesis. In a very real sense, both the null and directional research hypotheses are unsupported. This is termed the "double-whammy syndrome." Be prepared to explain why the directional difference found was in opposition to the directional difference which was originally hypothesized. Was the data unexpected, or was the original directional research hypothesis developed incorrectly? Perhaps neither, and the study represents merely an atypical outcome. In any event, study the results and data carefully and arrive at a logical explanation. Greater detail regarding the statistical testing of the null hypotheses is presented in Chapter VII, Statistical Analysis.

SUMMARY

Chapter III has described null, research, alternative, and alternate hypotheses. It has been explained that null hypotheses are the statistically tested

Hypotheses representing the "no difference" or "no relationship" condition. Research, alternative, or alternate hypotheses generally represent what the investigator is hoping to find in the study. The term "research hypothesis" is recommended. The research hypotheses are either directional (one-tailed) or non-directional (two-tailed), depending on whether or not a direction of expected difference or relationship can be ascertained.

Rules for developing hypotheses were presented in list form, together with a brief discussion regarding the theoretical aspects of testing (i.e., either rejecting or accepting) the null hypotheses. A suggested reading list has been provided. Checklist III should be completed before continuing to Chapter IV.

REFERENCES AND SUGGESTED READINGS

The list below has been selected with the utmost care. The listing has been purposely limited to only those texts which are of a great practical and useful value to most doctoral or professional researchers. Not every entry may be still in print, but generally a search to locate such a book will be very worthwhile. Entries denoted with a double asterisk (**) are those highly recommended for the topic specified. Parenthetical comments for each entry are added by this author.

Fox, D. J. The Research Process in Education. New York: Holt, Rinehart and Winston, Inc., 1969.

(A good general purpose text in this area.)

**Kerlinger, F. N. Foundations of Behavioral Research, 2nd ed. New York: Holt, Rinehart and Winston, Inc., 1973.

(An excellent discussion of hypotheses in Chapter 2, pp. 16-27.)

Tuckerman, B. W. Conducting Educational Research, 2nd ed. New York: Harcourt Brace Jovanovich, Inc., 1978.

(A very good presentation on constructing hypotheses; see pp. 20-35 particularly.)

CHECKLIST III

( ) 1. Understand the terms null, research, alternative, and alternate hypotheses. Test yourself repeatedly!

( ) 2. Recognize the difference between a directional (one-tail) and non-directional (two-tail) research hypothesis.

( ) 3. Satisfactorily complete Worksheet 3.1.

( ) 4. Use the Hypothesis Development Rules to develop your null and research hypotheses.

( ) 5. Share your null and research hypotheses with your advisor as soon as possible. No exceptions!

( ) 6. Understand the theory of accepting or rejecting the null hypothesis.

( ) 7. Review suggested readings and comments.

Evaluating Research Designs

INTRODUCTION

Chapter 4 will review design development considerations in detail. The researcher will ultimately design and then critically assess their project by using the included examples and worksheets.

UNDERSTANDING EXPERIMENTAL RESEARCH DESIGNS

There are generally two types of formal design types: descriptive, and experimental. Descriptive studies attempt merely to describe data; no inferences to a larger group or population can be derived from the analysis. (See Understanding Descriptive Research Designs, ahead.) Moreover, using a little thought and creativity, most research efforts can be designed to form some type of experimental design.

Why is this important? An experimental design approach will allow an objective, scientific analysis of the project's findings. The experimental approach necessitates hypotheses and statistical analysis. The result is usually a more professional and scientific study.

What constitutes a good experimental design? There are a number of formalized experimental research designs widely accepted in academic and professional applications. Generalized research design textbooks have come and gone, but one book is still regarded by most professionals as the definitive sourcebook; that authored by Campbell and Stanley (1963). In addition to presenting sixteen experimental-type research designs, Campbell and Stanley concisely describe twelve specific threats to design validity. Obtain this small book and read it!

UNDERSTANDING DESCRIPTIVE RESEARCH DESIGNS

Suppose no matter how the research topic is

considered or reconsidered, the study still appears descriptive rather than experimental. Then do it that way, but consult with the advisor for approval before continuing. Also, be certain that the study's null and research hypotheses do not make any statements of comparison regarding the data (or information) collected. Your research work will be considered descriptive and not experimental. Although experimental studies are preferred, a good descriptive study is far better than a poor experimental one.

DEVELOPING AND EVALUATING
YOUR RESEARCH DESIGN

No matter what form of research design the study finally takes (preferable experimental), <u>evaluate it by the following Nine-Point Design Danger List</u>:

1   <u>See the hypotheses/design relationship</u>. In reiterating a segment of the discussion found in Chapter III, hypotheses are the basic foundation of the research effort. Thus, the relationship between the study's design and hypotheses is a most critical one. Ensure that the research design will logically allow for the types of statistical comparisons needed to evaluate the data properly (much more about this in Chapter VII).

<u>Snap Quiz</u>: In less than five minutes, try explaining your research design and research hypotheses to a knowledgeable friend or peer. If you can't do it, the hypotheses and design need more work!

2   <u>Avoid complex group strata</u>. Suppose there are five different schools (groups) in a study. It is initially decided to evaluate the differences between males and females in each of those five schools; so there are ten groups (five schools multiplied by two sex groups). Next, an advisor says, "Let's analyze it by school, sex and 12 grades"; now there are 120 groups (five schools multiplied by two sexes multiplied by 12 grades)! A statistical test now has to attempt to evaluate those 120 groups. Obviously, every time a stratification variable, such as school, sex, or grade, etc., is built into an analysis, the groups tested are further subdivided.

It is much more powerful and professional to test 10 groups of 100 students each, than to test 100 groups of 10 students each. It is quite simple to end up with a great sounding design that will simply not work in practical terms! Minimum group size for respectable statistical testing is in the 30 to 40 respondent range. Drop below this level of respondents per group and statistical power will suffer.

3   Estimate attrition (subject drop-out). Attrition almost always happens in even the best studies. The more time-dependent the design is, the more attrition is going to become a factor. The research may result with a poor "n" size in each group ("n" symbolizing the number of subjects in your study). Low "n" sizes mean weakened statistical tests and that means potential trouble when testing the null hypotheses. Nothing could be more serious.

4   Consider issues of subject confidentiality or anonymity. In almost every research endeavor involving human subjects, issues of respondent confidentiality need strong consideration, and rightfully so. Commonly, identification numbers are needed for data editing and tabulation. Use random digits or a respondent-supplied number (such as those used in "secret witness" police or newspaper programs) to identify human subjects. Avoid using social security numbers, plant or school numbers, birth dates and, obviously, names. If feasible in your design, avoid the entire confidentiality issue completely and instead make responses anonymous.

Never gloss over confidentiality issues in research endeavors. Ensure that respondents totally understand that their answers are either confidential or anonymous. The respondent's understanding of this aspect not only provides better data for the study, but actually is a researcher's ethical responsibility to those surveyed.

5   Watch for the "Practice effect." This can be a common problem if the research design involves both pre- and post-tests. "Practice" on the pre-test may influence the post-test results and thus, the treatment effect can be erroneously assessed. Campbell and Stanley (1963) had also addressed this issue and termed it "testing." If identical pre- and post-tests are used, some subjects may even remember correct responses to a cognitive pre-test and simply apply this information on the post-test. Thus, it is not the effect of the treatment

(or lack of treatment) that has had an influence on the post-test scores, but merely memorization.

Also, even if pre- and post-test questions are different, just the mere experience of taking a pre-test could affect the post-test scores for experimental or control groups, or both. Campbell and Stanley had also addressed this issue as "reactive effect of testing." This effect is also known as "becoming test-wise." Evaluate your design carefully regarding these potential hazards.

6   Beware the "Hawthorne effect." Will subjects react differently in a study if they realize that they are being watched? In an experiment years ago, workers demonstrated different skills and abilities simply by virtue of the fact that they were being studied. The experiment was conducted at the Hawthorne plant of the Western Electric Company, where this effect was first recognized. (See G. Homans, "Group Factors in Worker Productivity," in H. Prohansky and B. Seidenberg, Eds., Basic Studies in Social Psychology. New York: Holt, Rinehart and Winston, 1965, pp. 592-604.) Evaluate your design carefully to ensure that the Hawthorne effect can be avoided, or at least minimized.

7   Evaluate logistics and time. Think about various logistics problems which may be encountered by the research design. If the research involves many locations, will travel be a substantial expense? Will it be difficult to monitor data collection activities at numerous locations? Are field supervisors needed, and at what expense?

Whenever in doubt, reduce the physical distances and time frames involved in the research effort, and take this action early in the project. Don't ignore potential logistic and time problems. These elements always seem to reappear and cause severe complications after the design is firmly set and the data begins to come in. In dissertations particularly, logistic and time problems can be devastating to the overworked and underpaid student.

8   Review and budget the economic factors. A problem can quite easily develop within the economics of an innocent looking doctoral dissertation or professional

research effort. It is very wise to review all potential expenses and adjust them upwards a minimum of 25%. Modify the research design to accommodate the estimated budget; once a design is implemented, it is generally too late to start cutting costs without reducing quality. See Table 4.1 and Worksheet 4.1 for a helpful guide to cost budgeting the study.

9   Review the Campbell and Stanley (1963) 12 threats to validity if the design is experimental. No matter what form of experimental design is arrived at, evaluate it in terms of each of Campbell and Stanley's twelve threats to research design validity as described in their text.

        Obviously, the above Nine-Point Design Danger List requires very critical review. If any potential problem areas cannot be resolved, this should be discussed openly with the advisor as a limitation of the study.

```
DOCTORAL MORAL III

If attempts are made to cover up the research
design flaws, per the Nine-Point Design Danger
List, you are now officially on thin ice!
```

SUMMARY

        Chapter 4 discussed the evaluation of research designs. The concluding Nine-Point Design Danger List was presented as a guide to developing and evaluating such designs. Checklist IV further summarizes the chapter. Complete this checklist before proceeding, and also review the suggested reading list which follows.

TABLE 4.1

COST ESTIMATES—EXAMPLE

Literature Searches	$ 50.00
Typing	420.00
Clerical	180.00
Printing - Questionnaires	175.00
Printing - Report	95.00
Postage - Questionnaires	20.00
Travel	40.00
Consultants	75.00
Keypunching	180.00
Computer Time	50.00

	Initial Estimate	$1,285.00
	Add 25% Adjustment	321.00
	FINAL ESTIMATE WITH ADJUSTMENT	$1,606.00

WORKSHEET 4.1

COST ESTIMATES

Literature Searches $_____

Typing   _____

Clerical   _____

Printing - Questionnaires   _____

Printing - Report   _____

Postage - Questionnaires   _____

Travel   _____

Consultants   _____

Keypunching   _____

Computer Time   _____

_____   _____

_____   _____

_____   _____

                                                         _____

                    Initial Estimate $_____

                    Add 25% Adjustment   _____

                                                _____
                    FINAL ESTIMATE
                    WITH ADJUSTMENT $_____

REFERENCES AND SUGGESTED READINGS

The list below has been selected with the utmost care. The listing has been purposely limited to only those texts which are of a great practical and useful value to most doctoral or professional researchers. Not every entry may be still in print, but generally a search to locate such a book will be very worthwhile. Entries denoted with a double asterisk (**) are those highly recommended for the topic specified. Parenthetical comments for each entry are added by this author.

Best, J. Research in Education, 3rd ed. Englewood Cliffs: Prentice-Hall, 1977.

(A good presentation on overall designs and experimental validity; see pp. 90-115 particularly.)

**Campbell, D. and Stanley, J. Experimental and Quasi-Experimental Designs for Research. Chicago: Rand McNally, 1963.

(The definitive text on experimental research design!)

Fisher, R. A. The Design of Experiments, 3rd ed. London, England: Oliver and Boyd Ltd., 1942.

(The classic book on design; written a long time ago, but the principles still hold true.)

**Kerlinger, F. N. Foundations of Behavioral Research, 2nd ed. New York: Holt, Rinehart and Winston, Inc., 1973.

(A logical and easy to read description of designs and experimental validity. In particular, see pp. 300-377.)

Webb, E. J., Campbell, D. T., Schwartz, R. D., and Sechrest, L. Unobtrusive Measures. Chicago: Rand McNally College Publishing Company, 1966.

(A book describing ways to collect data (i.e, observe human subjects), without creating Hawthorne effects.)

CHECKLIST IV

( ) 1. Understand the difference between experimental
         and descriptive research designs.

( ) 2. Decide which form of research design is to be
         utilized.

( ) 3. Carefully utilize the <u>Nine-Point Design Danger
         List</u> to evaluate your research design. Dis-
         cuss the design characteristics with your
         advisor.

( ) 4. Complete Worksheet 4.1 to estimate the research
         design cost factors. Use the 25% upward
         adjustment suggested.

( ) 5. Review the suggested readings and comments.

Instrumentation and Testing

INTRODUCTION

The hypotheses and overall design characteristics are only as good as the actual data collected. An instrument collects data and may be any form of published or original cognitive test, survey form, attitudinal or opinion survey, unobtrusive measuring device, or other type of measuring tool. All instruments, no matter what form they may take, must be considered and selected for use in terms of their data collection validity, reliability, and practicality factors.

Chapter 5 will initially review test instrument terminology. Following this, a section on other special considerations and potential problem areas regarding survey forms will be presented. Guidelines for both selecting a published instrument and developing an original instrument will also be presented. Next, a detailed study of the use of item analysis is discussed. Lastly, a summary and chapter checklist will be presented.

VALIDITY AND RELIABILITY
INTRODUCTION

Consider a clock that sometimes runs fast and other times runs slow, with no pattern as to its running speeds. Such a clock does not measure what it is supposed to measure; namely, time—thus, the clock is not valid. Further, the clock doesn't measure time consistently, since the running speeds always vary. Thus, the clock is not reliable.

Naturally, a clock that is unreliable in running speeds cannot possibly give valid time. But what about a clock that is always exactly five minutes fast? Such a clock would not be valid, since the time would always be wrong (five minutes fast), but the clock would be reliable, since it would measure the time consistently.

In summary, if any instrument is valid, it must be reliable. If any instrument is reliable, it may or may

TABLE 5.1

A CLOCKWORK EXAMPLE—

VALIDITY AND RELIABILITY

Actual Correct Time		A Valid & Reliable Clock	B Not Valid But Reliable Clock	C Not Valid & Not Reliable Clock
5:00 PM		5:00 PM	5:05 PM	6:30 PM
5:30 PM		5:30 PM	5:35 PM	7:08 PM
6:00 PM		6:00 PM	6:05 PM	7:29 PM
6:30 PM		6:30 PM	6:35 PM	8:06 PM

Key:

Clock	Comments
A	Always correct (valid and consistent)
B	Consistent, but wrong (always five minutes fast) (not valid, but reliable).
C	Inconsistent and wrong (times vary) (not valid and not reliable).

not be valid. Try explaining the clock example to someone else. Review Table 5.1 for "A Clockwork Example."

VALIDITY

The purpose of this presentation is to describe
common forms of validity measures with clear and concise
definitions. The vast subject of validity is, by no
means, exhausted by this presentation. Researchers requiring additional information are encouraged to use the
Reference and Suggested Readings list supplied at the
conclusion of the chapter.

All research instruments must first be considered
in terms of their validity. The term "validity" simply
refers to the question: "Does the instrument measure
what it is supposed to measure?" In other words, as a
highly exaggerated example, a 7th grade algebra test
which contained test items regarding the history of the
Civil War would surely not be a valid test of 7th grade
algebra skills!

In a more real-life sense, issues of validity are
rarely so clear-cut. Many times it is difficult to
ascertain if test or survey items are, in fact, germane
to the subject area under investigation. A number of
formal methods for accurately evaluating instrument
validity are presented in the following discussion.

Very basically, there are three common forms of
instrument validity: content, criterion-related, and
construct. Table 5.2 graphically summarizes these types
of validity.

Content Validity

Content validity is a starting place for validity
assessment. Content validity is a logical (not mathematical or empirical) form of validity evaluation. It
consists of logical thought and judgment as the method
to derive valid test or survey items. As an example, a
5th grade teacher may compose a science test for students
on a monthly basis. The test items are selected by the
teacher on the basis of the teacher's logical judgment.
There is no quantitative evidence to objectively and
scientifically demonstrate the instrument's validity;
only the teacher's opinion. In more sophisticated situations, a test designer may begin with an original

TABLE 5.2

FORMS OF INSTRUMENT VALIDITY

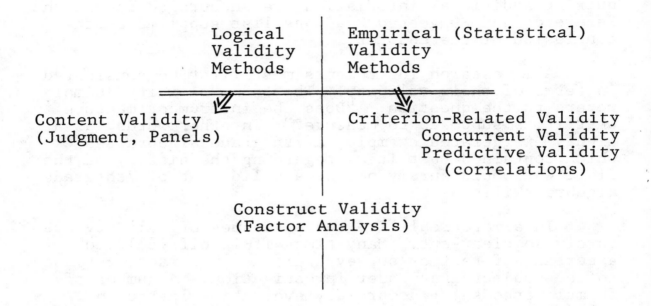

Note that content validity is a logical approach to validity, while criterion-related validity is empirical. Construct validity is a combination of logical and empirical approaches as utilized in factor analysis. Procedures used for each validity type are shown in parentheses. A more detailed discussion of each type of validity follows.

instrument as described above, but then receive additional test item assessments from other experts in the field.

Occasionally, formal panels of judges will logically evaluate and quantitatively rate instrument items independently and items may be added, modified, or dropped, relative to the panel's majority opinion. This final method is the strongest form of content validity, but is still largely dependent upon the quality of the judges and the integrity of the panel design and format. Nonetheless, when given a choice, the judging panel method is advised over the other content validity techniques.

Overall, content validity, while certainly hard to defend quantitatively, can be very valuable in certain research situations. The shortcoming of the content validity technique is that it is generally not very scientific in its approach. In using content validity, objections could be raised over a lack of objective data to conclusively support item relevancy. Often, other validity methods are utilized, either in conjunction with content validity, or on their own, in order to more quantitatively address the validity issue. Examine Table 5.4 for further information.

Criterion-Related Validity

Criterion-related validity is a method by which empirical measures, in the form of correlation coefficients, are established for the instrument(s). There are two common types of criterion-related validity:

    1   Concurrent Validity, and
    2   Predictive Validity

Both of these validity types utilize statistical correlation to arrive at a value or "validity coefficient" for the instrument. The correlation may range from 0.0 to +1.00. The closer to +1.00 the correlation coefficient is, the stronger the criterion-related validity.

Where does the correlation coefficient come from? A science teacher may initially use content validity (with or without a judging panel) to develop the test items, then test subjects twice, using both the teacher-made test and perhaps a published, standardized test instrument. If the teacher-made test is in fact a valid test, scores from subjects on this test should closely be related (i.e., be statistically correlated) to test scores derived from the standardized published instrument. Such a process represents the concurrent validity form of criterion-related validity. The validity of the teacher-made instrument was assessed concurrently by a correlation with a standardized, published instrument (the criterion).

Next, consider a situation in which the same science teacher collects data over a series of semesters and notices that students who tend to do well on a teacher-made 5th grade test tend to also do well (e.g., receive high grades) in 6th grade tests. Eventually, again using correlation techniques, the teacher may find that, within certain statistical error limits, a student's future test scores in 6th grade may be predicted simply by the 5th grade teacher-made test. In this case, predictive validity, this time in the form of a correlation coefficient between subjects' 5th grade test score and their test scores in later grades (the criterion), establishes the statistical measure. Likewise to concurrent validity, predictive validity also yields a correlation coefficient. The closer the coefficient value to +1.00, the higher, and better, the predictive validity of the instrument.

ACCEPTABLE CRITERION-RELATED VALIDITY COEFFICIENTS

A common student question: "What is an acceptable validity (correlation) coefficient, if criterion-related validity is used?" The following table (5.3) should be used as a practical guide only. Different experimental situations, subject matter, respondents, and instruments can all slightly modify the ratings shown.

In Table 5.3 note that both concurrent and predictive validity types of criterion-related validity are similar. Both use a criterion measure and correlation coefficient as a means of empirically establishing the validity of an instrument. However, one serious potential problem may still remain: how can one be sure that the criteria with which the new test is correlated to is in itself a valid index? In other words, a high concurrent validity between the teacher-made test and a published, standardized test could be indicating that both tests are equally poor, as opposed to equally

good! Likewise, a high predictive validity may be based
on improper indexes of future "successful" outcomes.
Use caution!

TABLE 5.3

REASONABLE VALIDITY COEFFICIENTS RANGES FOR
CRITERION-RELATED VALIDITY MEASURES

+1.00 to +.90 -------------------- excellent

+ .89 to +.85 ------------------------ good

+ .80 to +.84 ------------------------ fair

+ .79 or less ------------------------ poor

Hence, the quality of all criterion-related validity measures relies heavily upon the quality of the
criterion measure. Although criterion-related validity
is statistical and objective, it obviously may be seriously flawed. Researchers must use extreme caution
when selecting an appropriate criteria measure for use
with concurrent or predictive validity techniques. Thus,
the following doctoral moral:

DOCTORAL MORAL IV

Criterion-related validity is a very useful
empirical approach, but only if the criterion
itself is valid.

Review Table 5.4 for additional information on criterion-related validity techniques.

Construct Validity

Perhaps the highest form of validity is construct validity. Its development is generally credited to the field of psychology. Construct validity uses both the logical approach of content validity, coupled with the empirical approach of criterion-related validity.

Construct validity, in its true sense, utilizes multivariate factor analysis to develop factors (or constructs) within each test or survey instrument. For example, in an instrument measuring self-esteem, 150 original survey questions or items may be factor-analyzed into five specific factors (or constructs) of self-esteem. Thus, the instrument items will be categorized into five constructs. The process of developing factors is largely quantitative (using factor analysis), but also requires some substantial subjective decision-making on the part of the test author or researcher. The results from this multivariate method can be very rewarding, given the right situation.

Construct validity by nearly any standard is a powerful and sophisticated approach to instrument validity. The factor analytic procedure generally allows the researcher to view new insights into the quality of the test items and the interrelations between the questions. The approach is best used when numerous questions are involved (ideally, all having the same response scale), and many subjects are used in the research. Refer to Table 5.4 for more information regarding construct validity. A more detailed discussion of factor analysis may be found in Chapter VII.

RELIABILITY

As described previously, validity concerns the instrument's ability to measure whatever it is supposed to measure. Reliability evaluates the consistency of the measurements. As was discussed earlier, an instrument could be reliable but still not valid, yet every valid instrument must be reliable (see Table 5.1 for a quick review).

TABLE 5.4

INSTRUMENT VALIDITY SUMMARY

Form of Validity	Good Points	Poor Points
CONTENT VALIDITY Logical	*relatively easy to implement *no statistical knowledge required *fast *economical *easily understood	*not quantitative *process depends on individuals involved (author of test and/or judges)
PREDICTIVE/CONCURRENT VALIDITY (CRITERION-RELATED) Empirical	*statistical objectivity *widely used, understood, accepted *relatively easy, statistically *fast (if concurrent) *can be economical, depending upon number of subjects	*quality of statistics depends on criteria used *can take a long time to establish results (if predictive) *can be costly, depending upon number of subjects
CONSTRUCT VALIDITY Logical and Empirical Combination	*extremely sophisticated statistics to reveal factors (or constructs) *relatively fast results using analysis by computer *represents excellent combination of logical and empirical methods	*requires many questions, many subjects *difficult to learn and explain *not always well understood by audience *requires some subjective (opinionated) interpretation *can sometimes be costly due to large samples and computer time needed

Most reliability measures can be applied to either achievement or attitudinal instruments, however, reliability measurements are generally utilized more frequently and successfully in the former case. Attitudinal test reliability measurements are commonly harder to assess, since attitude is generally less consistent than aptitude. Nonetheless, reliability assessment should be ascertained with attitudinal instrumentation as well as with achievement tests, but perhaps viewed with greater leniency by the researcher.

Reliability measurements are presented as correlation coefficients. The higher the correlation value, the more reliable the instrument. As with validity, correlations may range from 0.0 to +1.00. A correlation of +1.00 represents perfect reliability within an instrument; conversely, a reliability of +.20 would reflect a quite unreliable instrument.

Some common reliability assessment techniques are test-retest, split-half, equivalent forms, KR-20, KR-21, and Hoyt's. All of these methods involve either correlation or analysis of variance procedures. Each of these common reliability measures will be presented and discussed individually, with a summary chart provided in Table 5.5.

Test-Retest Reliability

Test-Retest is a form of reliability measure which is fairly self-explanatory. A test instrument is simply administered twice to the exact same group of subjects with a short time lapse between testings. Theoretically at least, the subjects should each receive the identical scores both times, if the test is consistent (i.e., reliable). A correlation coefficient is simply calculated to measure the amount of relationship between subjects' first and second test answers. The correlation can be done either by item or, more commonly, by total test score.

Test-retest is usually an adequate method to determine instrument reliability, but it is not without its problems. Practice effects or other related troubles may create spurious results (see Special Considerations in Testing later in this chapter). The test-retest method is only recommended for use when other reliability methods are not feasible. Table 5.5 provides more detailed information.

62

Split-Half Reliability

The split-half reliability method is an improved variation of the test-retest procedure. Using split-half reliability involves first putting all test items in order of difficulty (if a cognitive test) or by subject matter groupings (if an attitudinal test). Next, the test is simply split; usually by odd and even question numbers. Version A of the test will consist of question numbers 1, 3, 5, 7, 9, . . . etc., while Version B of the test will be comprised of question numbers 2, 4, 6, 8, 10 . . . etc. The splitting of the test is usually done easily by computer or by hand, after the test has already been given to the group of subjects.

The theory is that if the total test is reliable, students should have highly related (correlated) scores between the two versions; odd and even. Of course, the difficulty lies in assuming both odd and even versions are relatively equal in content and difficulty.

Split-half reliability does have the advantage of efficiency, speed, and low cost, since the total test is given to the subjects just once. Split-half reliability is not an appropriate method for timed tests. This type of approach is a reasonable method of evaluating reliability, depending upon how equally the total test can be divided, in terms of item similarity. See Table 5.5 for further descriptive detail on this method.

Equivalent Forms Reliability

This method is identical to the split-half method, except for a technicality. In the equivalent forms method, two completely separate but equal tests are created. The subject group is tested twice; once with each equivalent test. As in the case of split-half reliability, a correlation coefficient calculated from both test scores on all subjects will indicate the reliability of the tests.

The success of this method depends greatly on the true equivalency of the two test versions. Writing test items to match so closely can be much more difficult than it sounds. Also, the equivalent forms reliability method requires two separate administrations of the instrument, which all takes time and money.

Equivalent forms reliability can be recommended for use only if the researcher's item writing skills are not a problem. See Table 5.5 for further evaluative information.

KR-20, KR-21, Hoyt's (Internal Consistency) Reliability

These reliability measures (and others similar to them) utilize more sophisticated mathematics to derive reliability coefficients. Internal consistency reliability measures are strongly recommended for use in most situations.

In general terms, the methods all involve a process known as item analysis. The theory states that if each item on a test constitutes a mini-test in itself, a high scoring respondent on the total test should have every mini-test (i.e., test question) answered in the same high score direction. Likewise, a low scoring respondent on the total test should have every mini-test answered in the same low score direction. The "internal consistency" reliability of the total test is evaluated by this theory and accompanying formula. (Refer to the Item Analysis section, ahead in this chapter.)

Reliability measures can be obtained by this method quickly, since the test need only be administered once. Problems with this method involve test length requirements (i.e., the most test items, the better), and the method is not appropriate for quickly-speeded tests. Computers are generally required for the sophisticated reliability calculations. See Table 5.5 for further descriptive detail regarding internal-consistency reliability.

Reliability Summary

Reliability can take on still more forms! The purpose of the presentation here was to quickly describe common types of reliability measures, give clear and concise descriptions, and recommendations for use. The vast subject of reliability is by no means exhausted by the discussion presented here. Researchers requiring additional information are encouraged to use the Reference and Suggested Reading List at the conclusion of the chapter.

TABLE 5.5

INSTRUMENT RELIABILITY SUMMARY

Reliability Type	Good Points	Poor Points
TEST-RETEST	*Simple to use *easy to understand	*takes time for two testings *practice effect in respondents *costly
SPLIT-HALF	*one test administration *easy to understand	*could be difficult to split test *not advised for quickly-speeded tests
EQUIVALENT FORMS	*creates two separate tests	*takes time for two testings *hard to write equivalent test items *costly
KR-20, KR-21 HOYT (Internal Consistency)	*recommended for most situations *most sophisticated, mathematically *well respected *combined with item analysis, provides much evaluative information	*harder to understand and explain *generally requires computer for calculation *not advised for quickly-speeded tests

Sufficient Values for
Reliability Coefficients

Despite the reliability method utilized, investigators need to be able to evaluate the reliability (correlation) coefficients they obtain. The type of subject matter, testing process, subjects and test length should all be taken into consideration, as described in the top half of Table 5.6. As a rough guide, reasonable reliability coefficient ranges are presented in the lower half of the table.

ITEM ANALYSIS

Item analysis is a powerful evaluative tool. It is utilized for recognizing instrument weaknesses, for test scoring, and for calculating internal consistency reliability measurements. It can easily be included in a doctoral or other professional research effort and, in reality, should be done much more often. It can be applied to either cognitive or attitudinal instruments.

The basic idea of any item analysis is to evaluate each test item in terms of its response pattern within the group tested. This analysis generally involves a correlation calculation which reflects each test item's ability to discriminate between "high scoring" and "low scoring" subjects. Using this theory, a high scoring respondent should answer test questions consistently in the high scoring direction. If the correlation between scoring high on the total test and scoring high on one particular question is strong, the question must be a good one. Thus, using correlation figures for each item on the test allows the researcher to evaluate each item's effectiveness and consistency, in relation to the total test. Luckily, computer programs in package form are available to perform item analysis.

Given the myriad of item analysis computer packages, only one still stands out as clearly the best. LERTAP (developed in New Zealand) is a powerful and highly flexible computer package that will yield item analysis, test scoring, and an internal consistency reliability value, all in one process! As if that were not enough, the programming required is almost unbelievably easy. Additionally, no special test forms or data input formats are needed, and that in itself is a tremendous luxury, as any experienced researcher already knows.

TABLE 5.6

REASONABLE RELIABILITY COEFFICIENT RANGES

Conditions which tend to lower or spuriously alter reliability coefficients:

* attitudinal tests

* opinion surveys

* complex subject matter

* short test (less than 20 items)

* speeded tests

* young children (under 12 years) as subjects

* inconsistent test administration

* unusual factors in testing environment

* small sample size (less than 30 respondents)

Ranges of "r" in the ideal situation:

+.90 to +1.00 .... excellent

+.85 to + .89 .... very good

+.80 to + .84 .... good

+.70 to + .79 .... fair

+.69 or less .... poor

TABLE 5.7

LERTAP ITEM ANALYSIS

Explanation of Terms:

Item Number = Test Question Number

Option = Number of possible answers to a question.

WT = Weight given for correct answer choice (for cognitive instruments).

N = Number of responses by subjects to each possible answer.

P = Percentage of responses to each possible answer.

PB-ST & PB-TT = Point-Biserial correlation coefficient between item response score and the Sub-Test (ST, reading) or Total Test (TT) score for the group tested. The higher the positive value, the better the test item. The range of values: -1.00 to +1.00.

B-ST & B-TT = Same as PB-ST and PB-TT except that the Biserial correlation formula is used instead of the Point-Biserial correlation. Refer to Senter (1969), pp. 451-456, for an excellent discussion of when to use which correlation coefficient. (See References and Suggested Readings List at this chapter's conclusion.)

Means, ST & TT = Sub-Test and Total Test Mean Scores for the group, as related to each question's response pattern.

TABLE 5.7 (continued)

Interpretation of Example:

Using point-biserial correlations as related to the sub-test, item numbers 2 and 5 have the highest positive correlation; these are the most valuable items of the five questions shown. In other words, subjects who get these two questions "right," will tend to do well on the entire sub-test (reading).

Conversely, Question 4 demonstrates a situation in which subjects who tend to give the correct answer to the question actually tend to do worse on the entire sub-test. This is indicated by the negative correlation.

The internal consistency reliability measure was found to be +.81 for the 70-item total test.

TABLE 5.7

LERTAP ITEM ANALYSIS

LERTAP 2.0   SUMMARY ITEM STATISTICS

TEST NO 1   YOUR SCHOOL, GRADE 5. MS. TEACHER   SUBTEST 1   READING

ITEM NUMBER 1   COEFFICIENTS OF CORRELATION   MEANS

OPTION	WT	N	P	PB-ST	PB-TT	B-ST	B-TT	ST	TT
1	O	2	12.5	C	0.19	0.18	0.30	0.28	C	35.50	41.00
C 2	1	9	56.3	C	0.15	0.16	0.19	0.20	C	32.78	38.67
3	O	4	25.0		-0.15	-0.20	-0.21	-0.27		29.75	35.25
4	O	1	6.3		-0.29	-0.21	-0.58	-0.41		23.00	32.00
TOTAL		16									

ITEM NUMBER 2   COEFFICIENTS OF CORRELATION   MEANS

OPTION	WT	N	P	PB-ST	PB-TT	B-ST	B-TT	ST	TT
1	O	0	0.0		0.0	0.0	0.0	0.0		0.0	0.0
2	O	6	37.5		-0.19	-0.15	-0.25	-0.19		29.83	36.33
C 3	1	6	37.5	C	0.65	0.59	0.83	0.76	C	38.17	43.17
4	O	4	25.0		-0.51	-0.50	-0.69	-0.68		25.00	31.50
TOTAL		16									

ITEM NUMBER 3   COEFFICIENTS OF CORRELATION   MEANS

OPTION	WT	N	P	PB-ST	PB-TT	B-ST	B-TT	ST	TT
1	O	3	18.8		-0.21	-0.27	-0.31	-0.39		28.33	33.67
2	O	0	0.0		0.0	0.0	0.0	0.0		0.0	0.0
C 3	1	12	75.0	C	0.0	0.06	0.0	0.08	C	31.75	37.92
4	O	1	6.3		0.35	0.34	0.68	0.66		42.00	47.00
TOTAL		16									

ITEM NUMBER 4   COEFFICIENTS OF CORRELATION   MEANS

OPTION	WT	N	P	PB-ST	PB-TT	B-ST	B-TT	ST	TT
1	O	1	6.3		0.11	0.08	0.22	0.16		35.00	40.00
2	O	3	18.8		0.14	0.11	0.20	0.16		34.00	39.33
C 3	1	11	68.8	C	-0.18	-0.12	-0.24	-0.16	C	30.82	37.09
4	O	1	6.3		0.01	-0.02	0.02	-0.05		32.00	37.00
TOTAL		16									

ITEM NUMBER 5   COEFFICIENTS OF CORRELATION   MEANS

OPTION	WT	N	P	PB-ST	PB-TT	B-ST	B-TT	ST	TT
1	O	1	6.3		-0.40	-0.46	-0.78	-0.90		20.00	25.00
C 2	1	12	75.0	C	0.77	0.82	1.05	1.12	C	35.17	41.08
3	O	2	12.5		-0.51	-0.59	-0.81	-0.95		21.50	26.50
4	O	1	6.3		-0.29	-0.21	-0.58	-0.41		23.00	32.00
TOTAL		16									

LERTAP Courtesy: Larry R. Nelson, Ph.D.

TABLE 5.7 (continued)

NUMBER OF INDIVIDUALS = 16.00   NUMBER OF ITEMS = 70.00

MEAN   = 37.69   HIGHEST SCORE = 47.00

STANDARD DEVIATION   = 7.37   LOWEST SCORE = 21.00

SOURCE OF VARIANCE	D.F.	S.S.	M.S.
INDIVIDUALS	15.00	11.65	0.78
ITEMS	69.00	115.91	1.68
RESIDUAL	1035.00	150.79	0.15
TOTAL	1119.00	278.35	0.25

HOYT ESTIMATE OF RELIABILITY = 0.81

STANDARD ERROR OF MEASUREMENT = 3.17

LERTAP Courtesy: Larry R. Nelson, Ph.D.

71

Not every computer installation may have LERTAP available, but investigate around. LERTAP is worth trying to locate. If LERTAP is unavailable, ensure that the capabilities, requirements, and shortcomings of the other computer package chosen are known before starting the data collection.

As an example of interpreting an item analysis computer print-out, a LERTAP print-out is shown in Table 5.7. The example is an item analysis of an achievement test given to a group of 16 subjects. (In reality this sample size is too small, and is used here for explanatory purposes only.) A detailed item analysis is shown (only included in this example are the first five test questions). Note both high and low correlation values for the various test questions, as highlighted in the table. Following this, a summary of test statistics is presented, including an internal consistency (Hoyt) reliability coefficient.

Even if LERTAP is unavailable for use, review Table 5.7. The table serves as an excellent guide to exactly what a top quality item analysis should include, and also provides a good instructional exercise for those interested in learning about, and using, item analysis in their research.

SELECTING A PUBLISHED
INSTRUMENT

Having an understanding of validity, reliability, and item analysis, how should the researcher actually select an instrument for use? When is it best to use a published instrument, as opposed to an original instrument, in the context of doctoral or other professional research?

Why bother using a published instrument? Mainly due to its professional acceptance, assuming the instrument is credible. Validity, reliability, and perhaps even item analysis data will be available in a printed form within the test manual. The instrument has probably been piloted and revised throughout the years. Comparisons between your resulting data and past research will also be facilitated, if the instrumentation is identical or correlated to other similar published tests.

In practical terms to the researcher using a published instrument, defending validity and reliability issues should be easier as compared to a situation in which non-published instruments are used. Inventing one's own instrument can involve tremendous labor and cost in establishing validity, reliability, and item analysis statistics. Without such figures, the researcher is clearly in a tenuous position to defend an original instrument; and instrumentation is, after all, an intrinsic element of the entire project's ultimate quality.

When reviewing published instruments, use the following Published Instrument Five-Step Procedure:

1   Begin by going directly to a test source book. Depending upon the subject matter, the source books described in Table 5.8 provide useful examples. Note that the reference sources appearing in Table 5.8 can save literally hundreds of hours of hunting for the appropriate instrumentation. Remember to always check the dates of the source books being reviewed and utilize the latest versions available for each source book.

TABLE 5.8

PUBLISHED INSTRUMENT SOURCE BOOKS

Title: TESTS IN PRINT
         (Buro, O.   Highland Park, N.J.:   Gryphon
         Press, 1982.)

Comments: Very large selection; cognitive and atti-
            tudinal, updated yearly.

Title: MENTAL MEASUREMENTS YEARBOOK
         (Buro, O.   Highland Park, N.J.:   Gryphon
         Press, 1982.)

Comments: Very large selection; psychological, socio-
            logical, and emotional test specialties;
            updated yearly.

Title: MEASURES OF SOCIAL/PSYCHOLOGICAL ATTITUDES
         (Robinson, S. P. and Shaver, P. R.
         Institute for Social Research, University of
         Michigan, 1976.)

Comments: Fairly large selection (about 130 instru-
            ments); psychological, sociological, and
            emotional test specialties; particularly
            good for tests in alienation, self-esteem,
            values, morals, and related psychological
            issues.

Title: MEASURES OF OCCUPATIONAL ATTITUDES AND
         OCCUPATIONAL CHARACTERISTICS
         (Institute for Social Research, University
         of Michigan, 1976.)

Comments: Fairly large selection (about 70 instru-
            ments); job satisfaction, job-related values,
            leadership; vocational interest; occupational
            status and other related issues.

2   As was the case in literature reviews, a review of
      the most recent trade and professional journals is
recommended to ensure a complete published instrument
investigation. (Perhaps instruments were found during
an earlier literature review of previous research.)

3   If a published instrument can be located for your
      topic of interest, it is worth the effort to con-
sider it strongly but not blindly. The time spent investigating the instrument must be measured against the
time period involved in developing an original test,
which is generally the only remaining alternative.

4   Paramount in your consideration of a published
      instrument, ensure that validity and reliability
measures are available, with considerable statistical
detail included. This information is usually obtainable
from the test author, publisher, or manual. If validity
and reliability information is unavailable, become
suspicious.

5   Many times numerous published instruments which
      closely fit the topic to be studied may be avail-
able. In these cases, each instrument must be evaluated
individually across a consistent array of evaluative
parameters defining the "ideal" instrument. These parameters will all too commonly be the responsibility of
the researcher alone.

     The Instrument Evaluation Chart (Table 5.9) pro-
vides a guide to how multiple published tests can be
fairly and logically compared. Some evaluative parameters will be consistent, no matter what the subject
matter or instrumentation (e.g., validity, reliability);
others will vary depending upon the specific situation.
It is imperative, however, that all instruments be considered across all feasible parameters shown. Study
Table 5.9 and note how each specific instrument's qualities are listed across the table. Next, complete Worksheet 5.9 for the specific published instruments under
consideration in your study, if multiple published
instruments are available.

     After completing Worksheet 5.9, rank the tests in
order of their quality in relation to the ideal instrument defined earlier. Place each rank in brackets or

parentheses. The highest rank (best score) is "1." Each column should contain all ranks 1 through 5. Ties in ranks can be shown as an average (e.g., a tie at the 4th rank would result in two ranks of 4.5). The ranking operation may allow for a clearer comparison between the instruments on each specific parameter and in total.

On the basis of the completed worksheet(s), a logical decision over which, if any, published instruments to be used can be made. It is mandatory at this step that the advisor be aware of the final instrument choice(s).

DEVELOPING AN ORIGINAL INSTRUMENT

Although extremely rare, a research project may be so unusual, creative, or innovative that few, if any, published instruments are appropriate for use. Often, some research dictates the need for both published and original instrumentation used together. In any of these cases, the investigator must devise an original instrument. Such instrumentation can take the form of attitudinal questionnaires, cognitive tests, or even laboratory measurement apparatus. The original instrument must evolve from a scientific developmental process. Follow this 13-Step Developmental Process for Original Instruments, when using questionnaires applied to human subjects:

1   Review the most similar existing instruments.
Obviously, no existing instrument is available, but broadly similar instruments can always be found. Available instruments may not even measure the specific topic of your study, but they may yield some new ideas regarding question form, response scales, test length, calibration, and similar factors. If all else fails in a search for similarly written instruments, simply refer to the instrumentation source books listed earlier and review the many different types of tests in terms of their questioning, design, and response patterns. This will at least provide a rough idea of what professional questionnaires and items should look like.

In short, writing good instrument items is a difficult business! Volumes have been completed on the subject and more volumes are still needed. For additional information, consult References and Suggested Readings at the end of this chapter.

2   In writing original items, start by first listing
        one to five major concepts that are to be inves-
tigated by the instrument. Keep these major concepts as
autonomous as possible.

3   Weigh each major concept in importance; assign
        numerical values to these categories if possible.

4   Decide on a total number of questions desired; if
        in doubt, use a conservative (low) estimate,
usually 20 to 50 items. Remember to consider the respondent's interest level, attention span, and fatigue
factors when deciding on a questionnaire's length.
Estimate, using the previous weights (step 3 above),
how many questions need be developed for each major concept within the instrument. The more important major
concepts require more questions.

5   Write items individually, in question form, on
        3 x 5 cards. Code each item's major concept cate-
gory in the top right-hand corner.

6   Develop response scales for each item. Try to
        stay consistent in types of response scales
utilized. For example, if using a Likert-type (e.g.,
five-point scale), use it consistently throughout the
instrument or test section. More about response scales
in the upcoming section.

7   Categorize all cards and read the items to a peer.
        Make corrections to eliminate ambiguous wording.
Combine similar items which ask the same, or similar,
questions.

8   Refine the number of items down to the originally
        estimated level.

9   Consider reversing the wording on a few (10-20%)
        of the final items. This reduces the "halo
effect," to be described later in this chapter.

10   Consider the item wording relative to vocabulary
        level of the intended respondents. Some intermed-
iate school districts have computer programs which will
review sample sentences and then output a reading index
in grade equivalent units. Alternately, consult with a
reading specialist at a local school or university. Do
not over-estimate or under-estimate the respondents in
their reading aptitude. Over-estimation of respondent
reading skills can cause item misunderstanding, misin-
terpretation, and lowered validity and reliability.
Under-estimation of respondent reading skills can cause
levity, insult, or even resentment regarding the instrument and even the entire study.

11   At this stage, the instrument must possess at
        least defendable content validity, using the
techniques described earlier in the chapter (with or
without a judging panel). An empirical approach to
validity could be optionally done at the formal pilot
testing stage, discussed later in this chapter.

12   Informally test the items for clarity with a very
        small group (minimum 20 subjects) similar to the
project respondent group. This step is not to be confused with the formal pilot testing to optionally be
completed later. This very small, informal testing
session regards item clarity only.

13   Formally pilot test the instrument. (For details,
        see Pilot Testing section ahead in this chapter.)

Response Scales

        Typically, in cognitive (i.e., achievement)
studies, open-ended "write-in" answers, true/false
questions, or multiple-choice formats are utilized. The
last two formats are generally recommended for doctoral
dissertations and other professional research, since
sample sizes tend to be large and computer analysis of
data is usually done.

Open-Ended Responses

        In cognitive or attitudinal instruments, the
researcher may be tempted to use the common "write-in"

answer response approach. Such methods are fine, within limits, but if the research design calls for statistical comparisons, tests between groups, or correlational studies, the resulting data collected from these response types will probably be inappropriate.

Nonetheless, open-ended questions can be of value in a study by representing the "human element" or qualitative aspect of a research project. Oftentimes open-ended responses give insights that no amount of statistical data could ever show. Use open-ended answering patterns for this purpose only, and do not expect to use results statistically. (Note that utilizing open-ended responses statistically can be done by reading all responses and coding them, but it is a huge job.)

Multiple-Choice Items

Regarding the writing of quality multiple-choice items, follow these five basic Multiple Choice Item Rules:

1   Keep multiple responses closely equal in length.

2   Avoid "none of the above" or "all of the above" type choices.

3   Consider "correction for chance guessing" adjustment factors in item scoring (if the instrument is cognitive).

4   Keep the question and all its responses clearly worded.

5   Consult the Suggested Reading List entries for more detailed item writing pointers.

Likert-Type Responses

If questions are attitudinal, the Likert-type scales are commonly used. Likert-type scales generally have five to seven response choices in degrees of progressive feelings (e.g., 1-strongly agree; 2-agree; 3-neutral; 4-disagree; 5-strongly disagree). Levels of agreement are commonly used, but, of course, other attitudes can be used with the scales.

TABLE 5.9

INSTRUMENT EVALUATION CHART

EXAMPLE

<u>STEP 1</u>

For this example, six criteria were established, as follows:

1. Have validity of .90 or higher (assuming credible method).

2. Have reliability of .85 or higher (assuming credible method).

3. Be recently developed.

4. Be for math students, aged 8-12 years.

5. Be short in length (approximately 30-40 items).

6. Take a short time to complete (approximately 20 minutes).

7. Item analysis data should be available.

8.

9.

10.

80

TABLE 5.9 (continued)

STEP 2

Evaluative Parameters

Criteria Number:	3		4		5		6		1		2		7		Rank Total
Tests	Date	Rank	For Ages	Rank	No. Items	Rank	Time	Rank	Validity	Rank	Relia-bility	Rank	Item Analysis	Rank	
A	1964	5	10-14	3	45	2	:20	1.5	.88	3	.73	3	yes	1.5	19
B	1969	3	10-16	4	50	3.5	:40	4	.81	4	.54	4	no	4	20.5
C	1967	4	8-12	1.5	40	1	:20	1.5	.73	5	.50	5	no	4	22
D	1978	2	9-16	5	75	5	:30	3	.93	1	.90	1	no	4	21
E	1981	1	8-12	1.5	50	3.5	:25	2	.90	2	.87	2	yes	1.5	13.5
F															

Result:

Test "E" should be selected, provided all parameters are given equal importance by the researcher.

81

WORKSHEET 5.9

INSTRUMENT EVALUATION CHART

STEP 1

The "Ideal" instrument should be (complete below):

1. Have validity of .90 or higher (assuming credible method).   REQUIRED
                                                                  PARAMETERS

2. Have reliability of .85 or higher (assuming credible method).

- -

3.   CONDITIONAL
                                                                  PARAMETERS

4.   (Depending
                                                                    upon
5.   research
                                                                    needs)
6.

7.

8.

9.

10.

82

WORKSHEET 5.9 (continued)

STEP 2

Criteria
Number: 1   2

Tests	Validity	Rank	Relia- bility	Rank		Rank		Rank		Rank		Rank		Rank		Rank		Rank Total
A																			
B																			
C																			
D																			
E																			
F																			

Evaluative Parameters

Result:

83

Regarding the writing of quality Likert-type items,
follow these four basic Likert-Type Item Rules:

1   Ensure that each statement is fully compatible with Likert-type scale responses. A strictly dichotomous question (e.g., yes/no) would not fit the Likert scale properly. Questions should be assessing degree in using Likert-type scales.

2   Scale about 10-20% of the questions in reverse direction. As an example, if using a 1 to 5 scale, with "5" representing "strongly agree," reverse this scoring occasionally and let "1" indicate "strongly agree" instead. Alternatively, keep the response scales in constant direction, but re-word some questions in reverse direction.

3   Do not alter response scale width within any one sub-part of an instrument.

4   Consult the Suggested Reading List entries for more detailed item wording pointers.

Specifically regarding Likert-type scales, next consider Table 5.10. In Scale A, the respondent would simply "agree" or "disagree" with a statement. It should be very easy to decide on a response, but the degree or emphasis of the response is forever lost. This is basically a "true-false" type item. The other extreme, Scale B, would certainly provide exacting information regarding response emphasis, but requires unrealistically high abilities of discrimination and judgment on the part of an average respondent. Realistically, maximum response width should be seven to nine units.

Scale C is a common compromise solution. Yet, in years of experience, this scale tends to have one distinct problem: respondents cling to the "not sure" choice (which the author has subsequently coined the "cop-out" syndrome). This commonly occurs on psychological, values, or morals questioning. Why does this matter? The importance of answering spread (i.e., statistical variance) in question responses relates to basic statistical theory and is critical to the resulting quantitative analysis.

Scale D eliminates the "cop-out" syndrome, while maintaining a good compromise in response width, usable with most respondents. It is considered a "forced decision" response format.

Scale E is a reduced width version of Scale C, and basically has the identical shortcoming—that of the "not sure" choice. Nonetheless, it must be stated that Scale E is, by far, the most common and traditional Likert-type scaling pattern in use today.

Scale F is a modified version of Scale E, eliminating the "not sure" choice, but providing only four levels of response discrimination.

Considering all six of the examples shown in Table 5.10, certainly none (except perhaps Scale B) are totally incorrect. Numerous modifications of these six scales have also been devised. The response scale choice largely depends on the age of the respondents, subject matter, statistical analysis, and overall research goals. Table 5.11 generally summarizes an evaluation of the six Likert-type response widths shown. If planning on using Likert-type scales, evaluate the specific conditions of the study, review Table 5.11 and select scale width accordingly.

SPECIAL HAZARDS IN
INSTRUMENTATION AND TESTING

Aside from item writing and the selection and development of response scales, there are special hazards to be reviewed in instrumentation and testing. Consider the instrument (and research design) in terms of its relative susceptibility to these four Special Hazards in Instrumentation and Testing:

1   Beware the "Is this what you're looking for?" syndrome. Often, respondents are genuinely attempting to "help" the researcher. Perhaps respondents strongly believe in the project goals or research hypotheses, or maybe they personally know the principal investigator of the study. Often, the respondent knows what the answer to an attitudinal question "should be" for the research's sake, but doesn't really feel that way. Watch for responses which are aimed at satisfying the research or project goals instead of providing accurate and sincere evaluative data.

TABLE 5.10

LIKERT-TYPE RESPONSE WIDTHS

SCALE	STRONGLY DISAGREE	DISAGREE	NOT SURE	AGREE	STRONGLY AGREE
A	1--2				
B	1234567...----------------50-----------------100				
C	1-------2-------3------4------5------6-------7				
D	1-------2---------3--------4--------5--------6				
E	1----------2----------3----------4----------5				
F	1-------------2-------------3------------4				

TABLE 5.11

EVALUATION OF LIKERT-TYPE

RESPONSE WIDTHS

Scale	Width	Neutral Choice?	Recommended Uses in Attitude Surveys
A	2	no	*use true/false or yes/no question wording *respondents under 10 years of age *severely handicapped
B	100	yes	*no practical use; simply too wide for accurate response level discrimination; maximum width should be 7 to 9 units
C	7	yes	*respondents over 15 years of age *complex questions with wide response attitudes possible *where "not sure" choice may be desirable, but not overly expected
D	6	no	*respondents over 15 years of age *complex questions with wide response attitudes possible *where "not sure" choice is either not desired, and/or is highly expected

TABLE 5.11 (continued)

Scale	Width	Neutral Choice?	Recommended Uses in Attitude Surveys
E	5	yes	*respondents over 10 years of age *relatively simple questions with average spread in responses expected *where "not sure" choice may be desired, but not overly expected
F	4	no	*respondents over 10 years of age *relatively simple questions with average spread in responses expected *where "not sure" choice is either not desired, and/or is highly expected

2   Consider the "self-fulfilling prophecy." Are re-
       spondents answering attitudinal questions
honestly, or are they giving answers which reflect the
way they would like to see themselves? This occurrence
can be hard or often impossible to detect for certain,
but beware of its possibility. In studies involving
psychological motivations, or controversial topics (sex,
politics, religion), the "self-fulfilling prophecy" can
emerge easily and weaken the data tremendously.

3   Recognize the "halo effect." In studies which
       involve long checklists of evaluative questions,
this can become a common problem. Do not design
an instrument in which the respondent will need to
assess numerous attitudes over a very large number of
questions, using an identical response scale. In this
situation, there is a tendency for responses to lose
dispersion. As an example, the respondent may get into
a habit of evaluating all items as "4" on a 1 to 5 scale,
regardless of attitude toward the questions. This problem can be usually remedied by reversing the wording on
various items at strategic locations in the instrument.
Also, use sub-parts within the instrument or allow short
rest periods to help break up the test administration.
These remedies help keep the respondent out of undesir-
able habit-forming response patterns.

4   Beware of the "Hawthorne effect." Particularly in
       behavioral research, respondents may alter their
normal pattern or responses due merely to their knowledge of themselves being studied, and not to the experimental treatment. This, quite obviously, can produce
spurious results from data collected under such circumstances. This effect could be very hard to eliminate in
some studies, yet its threat as a potential hazard is
often large. The instrument should be as non-invasive
as possible. (See also the discussion of the Hawthorne
effect in the previous chapter.)

       It is recognized that each of the four special
hazards listed may be very difficult to control or eliminate from various instruments. Nonetheless, the researcher must be aware of their possible existence and
their potential threat to sound instrumentation. The
optimum time to investigate the possible existence of
these hazards, among other things, is during the formal
pilot testing of the instrument.

PILOT TESTING

The formal pilot testing of either a published or original instrument is generally the first process to be eliminated in a usually hurried research schedule. This is unfortunate, because much can be learned by pilot testing any instrument, regardless of its origins. In most studies this author has reviewed over the past five years, the vast majority of doctoral or professional researchers would have been better off in taking less time to actually collect data and more time pilot testing instead.

```
DOCTORAL MORAL V

A small volume of good data is worth much more
          than a large volume of poor data!
```

Make every attempt to make time for a formal pilot test. If the instrument is original, a pilot testing should be mandatory. The pilot test allows the researcher to review instruments, subjects, the four special hazards, and actual test administration, all in one operation, and simultaneously. In using a published or original instrument, something is always learned from the pilot test; that's a strong statement, but it's true!

Further, the pilot test gives the researcher an opportunity to empirically measure validity and reliability of the instrument. Reliability can be ascertained by any of the common methods described earlier in this chapter, with internal consistency reliability as the preferred method. If establishing criterion-related validity, the criterion test should be administered just before or after the actual project instrument. Remember that in the case of original instrumentation, the use of empirical validity and reliability measures are highly recommended. The amount of data collected is totally irrelevant if the instruments collecting the data are not valid and reliable.

How can a pilot test be evaluated? When pilot testing an instrument, seven specific indices should be investigated. Table 5.12 lists these common pilot test assessments and demonstrates such an evaluation. Use

Table 5.12 as a guide and then complete Worksheet 5.12 for your research. A poor pilot testing, due to any element(s) shown on Worksheet 5.12, may call for a total revamping of the instrument and new pilot testing at a later date. Before becoming too upset over that last statement, just consider the dire consequences of not finding out that the instrumentation or its administration is flawed until it is too late!

Upon an evaluation of a final pilot test, the instrument and its administrative procedure must be within an acceptable tolerance level to the researcher. Review the Pilot Test Final Evaluation Guide:

1   Validity and reliability measures must be within acceptable limits as outlined earlier in this chapter (refer to Tables 5.3 and 5.6).

2   If done, item analysis should have been completed with satisfactory results.

3   Special hazards (Halo and Hawthorne effects, Self-Fulfilling Prophecy, etc.) should be accounted for and evaluated as being at controlled and minimal levels.

4   Test administration and time of completion should all be within acceptable, pre-determined limits.

The testing instrument, be it a published or original entity, has now passed the major piloting indices and is finally ready for use as a professional evaluative tool.

SUMMARY

Chapter 5 has detailed issues concerning instrumentation and testing. Major topics discussed involved validity, reliability, item analysis, selecting a published instrument, developing an original instrument, special hazards, and pilot testing. Suggested readings are also provided. A Checklist, as usual, appears at the chapter's end and should be completed before proceeding to the following chapter.

TABLE 5.12

PILOT TEST EVALUATION—EXAMPLE

<u>INDEX</u>

Test Name: <u> COGNITIVE STATISTICS TEST </u>

Estimated Test Time: <u> - </u> hr. <u> 30 </u> min. <u> - </u> sec.

Pilot Sample Size: <u>   30   </u>   Date: <u> 7/24/82 </u>

Setting: <u> Classroom; graduate level </u>

Grade each: A (excellent), to E (very poor)

		Grade	Comments*
1.	Reading of instructions	B	✓
2.	Demonstration of form completion	A	
3.	Clarity of questions to respondents	B	✓
4.	Validity check done (r = +.91)		✓
	Type: <u> Concurrent </u>		
5.	Reliability check done (r = +.82)		✓
	Type: <u> Internal Consistency/LERTAP </u>		
6.	Actual test completion for sample group	B	✓
	Time: <u> </u> hr. <u> 35 </u> min. <u> 20 </u> sec.		
7.	Halo/Self-Fulfilling Prophecy/ Hawthorne Effects	B	✓

- -

TABLE 5.12 (continued)

*COMMENTS (refer to previous 7 points)

1. Teacher did not stress confidentiality issues enough. Add new sentences to describe why study is being done.

2.

3. Questions 3, 6, 9 and 11 were inquired about; 6 is ambiguous, 9 should probably be thrown out.

4. Concurrent validity established at +.91 using Fisher's Standard Statistics Test** (1967).

5. LERTAP analysis; item analysis reveals that item 9 should be removed.

6. Test took about 5-1/2 minutes longer than expected, but is within acceptable range.

7. Halo effect possible only on questions 3, 4 and 5. Possibly reverse wording on question 4.

** Fisher's Standard Statistics is a ficticious title.

93

WORKSHEET 5.12

PILOT TEST EVALUATION

<u>INDEX</u>

Test Name: _____

Estimated Test Time: _____ hr. _____ min. _____ sec.

Pilot Sample Size: _____ Date: _____

Setting: _____

Grade each: A (excellent), to E (very poor)

	Grade	Comments*
1. Reading of instructions	_____	_____
2. Demonstration of form completion	_____	_____
3. Clarity of questions to respondents	_____	_____
4. Validity check done (r = ____)		_____
Type: _____		
5. Reliability check done (r = ____)		_____
Type: _____		
6. Actual test completion for sample group	_____	_____
Time: ___ hr. ___ min. ___ sec.		
7. Halo/Self-Fulfilling Prophecy/ Hawthorne Effects	_____	_____

94

WORKSHEET 5.12 (continued)

*<u>COMMENTS</u> (refer to previous 7 points)

1.

2.

3.

4.

5.

6.

7.

REFERENCES AND SUGGESTED READINGS

The list below has been selected with the utmost care. The listing has been purposely limited to only those texts which are of a great practical and useful value to most doctoral or professional researchers. Not every entry may be still in print, but generally a search to locate such a book will be very worthwhile. Entries denoted with a double asterisk (**) are those highly recommended for the topic specified. Parenthetical comments for each entry are added by this author.

**Adkins, D. C. Test Construction, 2nd ed. Columbus, Ohio: Merrill Publishing Company, 1974.

(One of the few good and practical texts on actually writing instrument items.)

Chase, C. Measurement for Educational Evaluation, 2nd ed. Reading: Addison-Wesley, 1978.

(A good, general purpose textbook.)

Chun, K., Cobb, S. and French, J. Measures for Psychological Assessment. Ann Arbor: Institute for Social Research, 1976.

(A massive reference to psychological test instruments; designed very well for the user.)

**Ebel, R. L. Essentials of Educational Measurement. Englewood Cliffs, New Jersey: Prentice-Hall, Inc., 1972.

(A good text specifically in areas of instrumentation validity, reliability and item analysis; see pp. 383-447.)

Nelson, L. R. Guide to LERTAP Use and Interpretation. Dunedin, New Zealand: Education Department, Univsity of Otago, 1974.

(LERTAP source document.)

Robinson, J., Athansiou, R. and Head, K. Measures of Occupational Attitudes and Occupational Characteristics. Ann Arbor: Institute for Social Research, 1976.

(A limited, yet very good reference, listing some rather fine occupational attitude instruments.)

**Robinson, J. and Shaver, P. Measures of Social Psychological Attitudes. Ann Arbor: Institute for Social Research, 1976.

(A very complete reference volume, listing instruments categorized by topic of study. Some example instruments are also shown in many cases.)

**Senter, R. J. Analysis of Data. Glenview, Illinois: Scott, Foresman and Company, 1969.

(An excellent section regarding point-biserial and biserial correlations as used in item analysis; pp. 451-456.)

**Thorndike, R. and Hagen, E. Measurement and Evaluation in Psychology and Education, 4th ed. New York: John Wiley, 1969.

(A good book detailing instrumentation validity, reliability and item analysis.)

CHECKLIST V

( )   1. Understand the terms validity and reliability. Explain "A Clockwork Example" to a friend.

( )   2. Review the different forms of validity. Are you sure which form(s) will apply to your instrumentation?

( )   3. Review the different forms of reliability. Are you sure which form(s) will apply to your instrumentation?

( )   4. Recognize the value and power of item analysis. Seriously consider its use in your study.

( )   5. Understand the various advantages and disadvantages of using either a published instrument or your own original instrument.

( )   6. When reviewing published instruments use the described Published Instrument Five-Step Procedure; this also entails completing Worksheet 5.9.

( )   7. When creating original instruments, complete the 13-Step Developmental Process for Original Instruments.

( )   8. If using original or published instruments, review the various response scales in terms of their advantages and disadvantages. Make a decision on the response scale(s) desired.

( )   9. Review the four Likert-Type Item Rules, if this response type is to be utilized.

( ) 10. Understand the four Special Hazards in Instrumentation and Testing. Carefully evaluate instrumentation to be used with regard to these hazards.

( ) 11. Strongly consider instrument pilot testing. If pilot testing is done, complete Worksheet 5.12, then review the four-point Pilot Test Final Evaluation Guide.

( ) 12. Review the Suggested Readings and comments.

Sampling Techniques and Data Collection Methods

INTRODUCTION

Instrumentation has established the content and format of the questions to be answered, but exactly who is to be asked? Sampling techniques are quite varied and can often be extremely complex in their structure. Chapter 6 will concisely review the major types of sampling utilized in most dissertation and professional research work. Sampling technique, sample selection, common sampling problems, and sample size determination will all be individually discussed.

DEFINITIONS

Definitions of basic terms regarding sampling techniques described throughout this chapter are detailed here:

<u>Population</u> - The entire group of unit of interest in a research study (synonym: universe) (e.g., the population consists of all learning disabled children in the United States).

<u>Respondent</u> - An individual subject or single case of investigation in a research study. Technically, respondents could be people, animals, or data records from any source (synonyms: subjects, cases) (e.g., the test was given to 100 learning disabled respondents for completion).

<u>Sample</u> - A select group from the population chosen to represent this population. Samples can be scientifically or non-scientifically developed (e.g., a sample of learning disabled children was selected).

<u>Sample Size</u> - Usually expressed in percentage of the population, sample size indicates the relative numbers of those sampled from the respective population (e.g., a 10% sample size of learning disabled children was selected).

Throughout this chapter, it will be noticed that concepts are explained in terms of written instruments as applied to human subjects. Nonetheless, the reader should understand that instrumentation may take many forms (written documents, watches, meters, medical apparatus, etc.), and likewise subjects certainly need not be human. Nonetheless, the identical sample selection criteria and data collection methods to be discussed must still be applied to maintain necessary scientific accuracy.

COMMON METHODS OF SAMPLING

In this section, major sampling techniques as used in dissertations and professional research will be described. The reader should recognize that the presentation here is meant to be accurate and concise, but is limited in its concent. Researchers requiring more information on sampling techniques should consult the References and Suggested Readings section at the end of this chapter.

Random Sampling

Random sampling is perhaps the most popular sampling method in research work because it is easy to understand, relatively accurate, and reasonably quick to implement. Of course, random sampling methods do have their limitations, but their consistent value still makes them a common choice.

Random sampling actually consists of a few different techniques. In simple random sampling, a population listing or similar source document is available and sample respondents are simply selected, at random, from the population listing.

Systematic random sampling is a slight variation on simple random sampling. In this case, subjects are selected from a population listing in a systematic way (e.g., every tenth name on the population list is sampled). This method is fast and easy, but is accurate only if the listing of the population is not biased in any way (assuming the researcher is fully aware of all potential list biasing factors in the first place).

With either simple or systematic random sampling methods, beware of these potential problems:

1   Many times simple random sampling is not really so
     simple or random. Numerous forms of bias can dimin-
     ish the integrity of random selection.

2   Make sure that the sample size is adequate for good
     representation of the population (see Sample Size
     section, ahead). In most simple random sampling
     situations, if unsure of an appropriate sample size,
     use a sampling percentage which seems larger than
     needed. Simple random sampling has really never
     been known for its economy in sample size percent-
     age.

Stratified Sampling

A more sophisticated approach to sampling than
offered by simple random methods involves a family of
techniques known generally as stratified sampling.
These methods use known characteristics of the population subjects and select a sample (proportionate or dis-
proportionate), based upon these known characteristics
or strata. As an example, stratified proportion sampling with a 10% sample size on a population of 70 males
and 30 females, would yield a sample of 7 males and 3
females. The variable of sex would be the "stratifying
variable" upon which the sample is proportionately controlled. As a result, proper representation of the
sample to the population on this particular stratifying
variable (i.e., sex) has now been ensured.

Of course, much more complex strata can be simultaneously controlled in any one sampling design. Multi-
stage, stratified proportion sampling is a technique
utilized to accomplish this task. For example, stratas
of income, age, and sex for the population may be already known characteristics, and a sample can be
selected to ensure proportional representation on all
three of these strata simultaneously. Some very
sophisticated national studies can involve a great number of stratifying variables. In dissertations or other
professional research, two to five stratifying variables
are generally common ranges.

Not all sampling need be necessarily proportionate
to the stratifying variable percentages. Based on the
previous example, if a population of 90 males and 10
females was sampled with stratified-proportion sampling
of 10%, only one female would be sampled. This would
result in not enough females in the sample for accurate

statistical testing. To artifically increase female representation, use disproportional sampling instead.

If using either stratified-proportional or strati-fied disproportional sampling methods, beware of a major problem. The most common stratified sampling error in-volves the use of too many stratifying variables on inadequate sample sizes. In other words, samples can easily become broken down into strata which are too finely detailed for accurate statistical analysis. If a very small sample size in each strata results, findings or conclusions from these small strata can be very mis-leading. In rough terms, statistical tests require about 30 subjects for group category analysis. A multi-stage stratified sample may provide a precise represen-tation of a large population while utilizing a very small sampling percentage, but the number of subjects in each category of each strata must still be at or around this minimum of 30. As an example, for the stratifying variable of "sex," a minimum of 60 total respondents are required (30 respondents times two sex categories, male and female).

Obviously, much planning regarding statistical analysis and group category size must be pre-established before implementing a complex multi-staged stratified sampling method, but don't let the complexity be detouring. Stratified sampling methods can be extremely effective in studies involving both very large and extremely diverse populations. Seek additional consult-ing assistance if necessary to design such a sampling method if you feel the situation dictates the need. (Table 6.1 will help you evaluate possible stratified sampling needs.)

Cluster Sampling

Cluster sampling is the most economical method for collecting data from a large geographic area. Many times a cluster sampling technique will be coupled with a stratified sampling method in a national survey. In dissertations and most other professional research, cluster sampling is not often used.

In the cluster sampling technique, a larger geo-graphic boundary is loosely considered a respondent area. The entire sample is comprised of a collection of clus-ters, each chosen specifically on the basis of descript-ive factors. Clusters are delineated further by blocks or tracts. Field or phone interviewers will then concentrate on obtaining individual interviews from respondents within these clusters, blocks or tracts on either a complete basis or by using simple random or stratified sample selection techniques. More detail regarding cluster sampling may be found in books by the Survey Research Center (1972) and Sudman (1976).

Miscellaneous Sampling Techniques

A number of other sampling techniques are also commonly used (and misused) in research work:

Quota sampling simply involves getting certain respondents to participate in the study until a pre-established interview quota is met. As an example, a survey may call for 40 male and 30 female respondents. The researcher will very simply fill that quota. When the quota figures are met, the sample is completed. Quota sampling is a somewhat widely used, but not recommended, sampling approach.

Convenience sampling is occasionally used in newspaper or radio polls and market research in shopping malls. This technique simply uses as its sample any respondent that is willing and available. The method is obviously not scientific and is not recommended for dissertations or other professional research efforts.

Snowball sampling starts with a small number of random or non-random subjects and then, at the end of an interview, has each of these subjects recommend other potential respondents. Again, this procedure is not scientific and is not recommended for high quality research endeavors.

SELECTING THE OPTIMAL SAMPLING METHOD

How can the appropriate sampling methods be determined for any one particular research effort? Table 6.1 provides a useful guide to sample method selection. Each common sampling technique is listed across the top of the table. Seven critical sampling criteria are shown vertically at the left side of the table. Each of these seven major criterion will be individually described for clarity in the following listing. Take time and review the Seven Sampling Criteria; each must be clearly understood in order for Table 6.1 to be effective:

1   Population Size. Population size can be defined
        as the size of the group that the completed re-
search findings will be generalized toward. How much
generalizing of the study's findings is anticipated?
Are respondents thought to be very different in differing geographic locations?

2   Accuracy and Cost. Ideally, every researcher
        wants high accuracy in a sample at a very low
cost. It just does not work that way! What is important to resolve is the accuracy required versus the
inherent costs involved. Different sampling methods
can have very different costs.

3   Population Listing Availability. Many times the
        availability of a population listing will influence
the type of sampling method used. Such listings are
indeed mandatory for systematic random sampling, since
that method involves sequential selection of respondents
from a given list in the first place.

4   Geographic Area. In most cases, very large or
        widely spread geographic areas of study are best
handled by stratified or cluster sampling. Covering
such large or spread out areas by other methods is not
very efficient or economical. Conversely, small geographic areas will not require cluster sampling in most
cases.

5   Population Diversity. Diversified populations in
        terms of respondent background, age, race, sex,
socio-economic status, I.Q., etc., tend to demand more
complex sampling strategies, usually of the stratified
or cluster sampling methods. More homogeneous populations to be sampled may not require the precision
offered by the stratified or cluster sampling methods in
order to produce a representative sample.

6   Prior Knowledge of Population and Data Avail-
        ability. How much is actually known about the
population, in general? The more variables known about
a population, the easier it is to conduct multi-staged
stratified sampling, since these known characteristics
are utilized to determine the sampling strata. Conversely, if little information is available regarding

variables within the population, a less sophisticated sampling approach is dictated.

7   <u>Simple or Complex Research Issues</u>. A simple research study (e.g., small scale market research, individual classroom testing) generally does not mandate the precision and complexity of multi-stage or cluster sampling. More complex research issues (e.g., most behavioral studies, psychological/social research, etc.) will require greater precision in sampling methods.

In Table 6.1, various sampling techniques are rated on each of the above seven criterion. Notations (√) in the body of the table indicate sampling techniques that commonly best fit each criterion choice; exceptions are possible. Compare the criteria evaluation to your research needs and find the sampling technique(s) best suited for your own study. Circle all checkmarks going across Worksheet 6.1B as they apply to your study (see example in Worksheet (6.1A). Give highest consideration to the sampling techniques having the most checkmarks circled.

Obviously, the value of Table 6.1 and Worksheet 6.1B is dependent upon the researcher's ability to correctly and honestly interpret and evaluate the seven major criteria. Additionally, Table 6.1 is to be used as a helpful guide in assessing sampling choice, and not necessarily as the definitive "last word" for all research work. Use common sense in evaluating the sampling method decision, and ensure that the final sampling technique chosen is formally approved by an advisor before continuing further.

In cases of persistent indecision between two or more sampling methods, the hierarchy listing (Table 6.2) should be consulted. Give first consideration to the sampling methods appearing highest on the list.

DATA COLLECTION METHODS

Once the sample is determined, how should the data actually be collected? In most doctoral dissertations, either group-administered or mail-administered data collection methods are employed. In other types of professional research, the list must be expanded to include both telephone and in-person interviewing.

TABLE 6.1

CHOOSING THE OPTIMAL SAMPLING TECHNIQUE

Criteria	Simple Random	Systematic Random	Stratified Proportion	Multi-Stage Stratified Proportion	Stratified Dis-proportion	Multi-Stage Stratified Dis-proportion	Cluster	Quota	Convenience	Snowball
I. Population Size										
Less than 100	✓		(✓)		(✓)			✓	✓	✓
100 - 300		(✓)	✓	✓	✓	✓		✓	✓	✓
300 - 1,000		(✓)	✓	✓	✓	✓	✓	✓	✓	✓
1,000 or more							✓			
II. Accuracy and Cost										
Highest accuracy/high cost	✓	✓	✓	✓	✓	✓	(✓)			
Medium accuracy/med. cost	✓	(✓)	✓	✓	✓	✓		✓	✓	✓
Low accuracy/low cost	(✓)							✓	✓	✓
III. Population Listing Availability										
Available	(✓)	✓	✓	✓	✓	✓	✓			
Not available								✓	✓	✓
IV. Geographic Area										
Large (regions, states ...)	(✓)	(✓)	(✓)	✓	(✓)	✓	✓	✓	✓	(✓)
Medium (cities, counties ...)	✓	✓	✓	✓	✓	✓	✓	✓	✓	✓
Small (school, community ...)	✓	✓	✓	(✓)	✓	(✓)	✓	✓	✓	✓
V. Population Diversity										
High	✓	✓	✓	✓	✓	✓	✓	✓	✓	✓
Medium	✓	✓	✓	✓	✓	✓	✓	✓	✓	✓
Low	✓	✓	✓	✓	✓	✓	✓	✓	✓	✓
VI. Prior Knowledge of Population Characteristics & Data Availability										
Much known		✓	✓	✓	✓	✓	✓	✓		
Some known			✓	✓	✓	✓	✓	✓		
Little known	✓	✓					✓	✓	✓	✓
VII. Simple or Complex Research Issues										
Simple	✓	✓	✓	✓	✓	✓	✓	✓	✓	✓
Complex			✓	✓	✓	✓	✓	✓		

✓ indicates sampling techniques that commonly best fit the criteria described; exceptions are possible.

( ) indicates possible use, depending upon specific design characteristics.

(circle checks, as appropriate, for your research design)

WORKSHEET 6.1A

CHOOSING THE OPTIMAL SAMPLING TECHNIQUE

	Simple Random	Systematic Random	Stratified Proportion	Multi-Stage Stratified Proportion	Stratified Disproportion	Multi-Stage Stratified Disproportion	Cluster	Quota	Convenience	Snowball
Criteria	2	4	7	5	6	4	4	2	2	N
I. Population Size										
Less than 100										
100 - 300										
300 - 1,000										
1,000 or more										
II. Accuracy and Cost										
Highest accuracy/high cost										
Medium accuracy/med. cost										
Low accuracy/low cost										
III. Population Listing Availability										
Available										
Not available										
IV. Geographic Area										
Large (regions, states ...)										
Medium (cities, counties ...)										
Small (school, community ...)										
V. Population Diversity										
High										
Medium										
Low										
VI. Prior Knowledge of Population Characteristics & Data Availability										
Much known										
Some known										
Little known										
VII. Simple or Complex Research Issues										
Simple										
Complex										
	2	4	7	5	6	4	4	2	2	N

✓ Indicates sampling techniques that commonly best fit the criteria described; exceptions are possible.

( ) Indicates possible use, depending upon specific design characteristics.

WORKSHEET 6.1B

CHOOSING THE OPTIMAL SAMPLING TECHNIQUE

(circle checks, as appropriate, for your research design; add total circles per each technique; evaluate)

Criteria	Simple Random	Systematic Random	Stratified Proportion	Multi-Stage Stratified Proportion	Stratified Disproportion	Multi-Stage Stratified Disproportion	Cluster	Quota	Convenience	Snowball
I. Population Size										
Less than 100	✓		(✓)		(✓)			✓	✓	✓
100 - 300		(✓)	✓	✓	✓	✓		✓	✓	✓
300 - 1,000	(✓)	(✓)	✓	✓	✓	✓	✓	✓	✓	✓
1,000 or more							✓	✓	✓	✓
II. Accuracy and Cost										
Highest accuracy/high cost	✓	✓	✓	✓	✓	✓				
Medium accuracy/med. cost	(✓)	(✓)					(✓)	✓	✓	
Low accuracy/low cost	(✓)	(✓)						✓	✓	✓
III. Population Listing Availability										
Available	(✓)	✓	✓	✓	✓	✓	✓	✓	✓	
Not available	(✓)							✓	✓	✓
IV. Geographic Area										
Large (regions, states ...)	(✓)	(✓)	(✓)	✓	(✓)	✓	✓	✓	✓	✓
Medium (cities, counties ...)	✓	✓	✓	✓	✓	✓	✓	✓	✓	✓
Small (school, community ...)	✓	✓	✓	(✓)	✓	(✓)	✓	✓	✓	✓
V. Population Diversity										
High	✓	✓	✓	✓	✓	✓	✓	✓	✓	✓
Medium	✓	✓	✓	✓	✓	✓	✓	✓	✓	✓
Low	✓	✓	✓	✓	✓	✓	✓	✓	✓	✓
VI. Prior Knowledge of Population Characteristics & Data Availability										
Much known	✓	✓	✓	✓	✓	✓	✓	✓	✓	
Some known	✓	✓	✓	✓	✓	✓	✓	✓	✓	✓
Little known	✓	✓					✓	✓	✓	✓
VII. Simple or Complex Research Issues										
Simple	✓	✓	✓	✓	✓	✓	✓	✓	✓	✓
Complex			✓	✓	✓	✓	✓	✓	✓	✓

✓ indicates sampling techniques that commonly best fit the criteria described; exceptions are possible.

( ) indicates possible use, depending upon specific design characteristics.

108

TABLE 6.2

SAMPLING METHOD HIERARCHY

Highest Form	Multi-Stage Stratified (proportional or disproportional)
	Cluster
	Stratified
	Systematic Random
	Simple Random
Lowest Form	All Others

In case of indecision regarding sampling method selection between two or more possibilities, select the technique which appears highest in the above hierarchy.

All data collection methods have their strong and weak attributes. How does the researcher decide which data collection method to use? How do accuracy, cost, and time all relate to each of these methods? Before answering those issues, a quick review of data collection methods must be presented.

Group-Administered Data
Collection Instruments

The group-administered method of data collection is relatively accurate, low in cost, and traditionally accepted, particularly in educational (classroom) research. Very commonly, data is collected by the reseacher, classroom teacher, or other professional within a group setting. If data is collected by the researcher, caution must be exercised to ensure that biases do not result. On the other hand, the procedural elements of data collection by the researcher can be easily controlled and little reliance on others is necessary, which is almost always a distinct advantage over other data collection techniques requiring field workers to administer the instruments.

If the data is collected by classroom teachers or field-workers, the researcher's own potential bias is simply exchanged for another's. The researcher must take extra measures to protect the quality of the data collection by making certain that the instructions and time lines regarding the project are implemented exactly as desired. Alterations in these areas can create or promote serious invalidity into the research design.

Mail-Administered Data
Collection Instruments

Mail questionnaires have advantages of respondent privacy and convenience. They are also relatively low in cost to implement. Concerning studies in which economics is of particular importance, and time is of little consideration, mail-administered data collection can be used effectively.

There are disadvantages regarding mail data collection. Only interested persons will return the survey form and serious biasing can result. It is very time-consuming to follow up on non-respondents to promote returned surveys. Mail surveys have notoriously low

response rates. Mailing lists used for sampling may in-
herently be biased depending upon the source of the list.
As is obvious, plan on extra time and money to develop
and mail follow-up letters or postcards to persistent
non-responders. Make sure a generous portion of time is
built into the project time line for the return of completed surveys.

Concerning the instrument itself, instructions
must be absolutely clear on mailed questionnaires since
the respondent completes the form privately. Question
wording must be unambiguous and response scales, if
used, must facilitate an ease of answering. In summary,
instrumentation must be appropriate to the research, yet
very simple to understand and fill out by the respondent. The key to success in using mail questionnaires
involves meticulous planning of the instructions,
questions, response types, form layout, and follow-up
activities.

Telephone-Administered Data Collection Instruments

Perhaps the most popular form of business and
marketing research data collection, and at the same
time the least used in doctoral dissertations, is telephone surveys. Telephone-administered instruments
offer advantages of data collection speed and spontan-
eity, and large geographic coverage. Also, survey
questions or comments can be handled at once by a
trained interviewer, adding to the quality of the data
collected. Disadvantages include biasing due to phone
number lists, medium to high cost factors, and interviewer biases, although the first concern can usually
be eradicated by random digit dialing techniques.

Random digit dialing has become a popular telephone data collection technique. In this case, the area
code and first three numbers of the phone number (i.e.,
the "exchange") are established beforehand, based upon
the geographic location to be sampled. The final four
numbers of the phone number are then randomly picked by
the phone interviewer. Such a method avoids problems of
sampling bias due to increasing amounts of unlisted
phone numbers in most urban directories. If using this
technique however, be prepared to answer the respondent's
first question, "How did you get my phone number?" when
contact is made.

The quality and persistence of telephone interviewers is critically important. If using this method,
allow extra data collection time for re-contacting
unavailable respondents. Further, make an effort to
ensure that interviewer biases toward the study or
toward individual questions are kept minimal. Lastly,
a follow-up spot-check to validate interview completion
with a small sub-sample of respondents is usually a good
idea.

In summary, for research in which data collection
speed is important, and a large, geographically diverse
sample is required, telephone interviewing can provide
the viable solution.

In-Person Data Collection

Personal interviewing (e.g., door-to-door or focus
group interviewing), although once highly regarded by
most behavioral researchers, is little used today except
as supplements to larger-scaled studied. In-person data
collection offers advantages similar to telephone interviewing with the small addition of visual contact, but
large subtraction of data collection speed and economy.
The effective use of in-person interviewing depends
largely on the topic of research (since full anonymity
is impossible) and on the quality and experience of the
interviewer.

In the majority of doctoral dissertations, and
even for most other professional research applications,
these methods of data collection, at least for the major
portion of a study, cannot be recommended. However, as
a supplement to a larger sample previously interviewed
by more efficient means, in-person interviews can add
very meaningful dimensions when applied to a small sub-
group of the original sample (usually about 20 respondents or less).

A special form of in-person data collection is the
focus group. In this case, a small number of partici-
pants are selected, either by scientific or non-
scientific means, to take part in an evaluative and
informal discussion. The group is usually interviewed
by a qualified researcher or psychologist to gain
information regarding in-depth reactions and/or attitudes
specific to a research topic. Audio or video taping of
such groups is also common. A focus group could range in
size from only about 5 respondents to a maximum of
usually about 20. Focus group results are best used as

112

a meaningful human element supplement to the statistical findings of a research project, particularly in fields of behavior science or market research. Its use for major data collection within a professional research project is not recommended.

SELECTING THE OPTIMAL DATA COLLECTION METHOD

The doctoral or professional researcher needs to decide upon an appropriate data collection method for use. Table 6.3 presents each major data collection method vertically, and various criteria for selection listed horizontally on the left side.

Review the table carefully and evaluate your research project per the selection criteria. Note that each data collection method has distinct strong and weak points denoted by the grading system. Notice that no single data collection method is ideal for all research situations. Reflect upon the data collection method you have selected and review it carefully for limitations or potential hazards. Seek approval from your advisor for the method finally selected.

SAMPLE SIZE DETERMINATION

How many subjects need to be sampled to accurately reflect the population? This is, by far, the most common sampling question, but it is not always easy to answer, as there are numerous statistical and non-statistical approaches to the issue. The best practical text found on the subject is authored by Sudman (1976), as this text requires less statistical knowledge than most other sampling method books.

Unfortunately, the statistical processes for estimating sample size are not used frequently in doctoral dissertations or most other professional research. Usually not enough is known about the statistical variance within the potential sample or survey question responses. The simple fact is that, in the majority of cases, sample sizes are derived from either similar studies, advisor recommendations, or the researcher's own common sense.

Critically important in sample size determination is the cost factor, which can easily become a major

TABLE 6.3

CHOOSING THE OPTIMAL DATA COLLECTION METHOD

Major Criteria	Group	In-Person	Phone	Mail
1. Accuracy of data collection	A	A	C	C
2. Speed of data collection	A	C	A	D
3. Low cost of data collection	B	D	A-D*	C
4. Potential for interviewer biases	C	A	A	D
5. Anonymity of respondents	A-D*	D	A-D*	A
6. Clarity of questions	A	A	A	D
7. Potential for in-depth responses	D	A	B	D
8. Little supervision needed to maintain quality	A-D*	C	C	D
9. Response rate	A	A-C*	C	D

---

* Denotes a possible wide quality range, depending upon specific methods of design implementation.

Grading Scale:

A .... excellent
B .... good
C .... average
D .... poor

consideration, especially in doctoral dissertations. Remember that as sample size increases, so increases clerical tasks, red-tape, printing, phone charges, key-punching, and computing time.

```
+-------------------------------------------------------+
|                                                       |
|                  DOCTORAL MORAL VI                    |
|                                                       |
|   Sample a group large enough to give credibility     |
|   to the research, but small enough to handle.        |
|                                                       |
+-------------------------------------------------------+
```

In most dissertations, sample sizes of 60 to 300 are common, with most averaging about 200 respondents. The nature of the study dictates specific sample sizes within each dissertation or project. Remember that statistical tests will require a minimum of 30 subjects per group for comparisons.

Depending upon data collection methods used, practically all initial sample size estimates need to be adjusted upward to compensate for attrition (i.e., respondent drop-out), respondent refusal to participate, or other similar circumstances. Study Table 6.4 and use the prescribed upward adjustments on sample sizes for each of the listed data collection methods. Table 6.5 gives examples of actual sample sizes needed, relative to the data collection technique used, for a sample size of 200. Apply the adjustments as shown to your own research project.

TABLE 6.4

SAMPLE SIZE ADJUSTMENTS

<u>Type of Instrument</u>	<u>Add</u>
Group	10%
In-Person	10-20%*
Phone	25%
Mail	60-100%*

---

* Range is largely dependent upon follow-up strategy.

TABLE 6.5

SAMPLE SIZE ADJUSTMENTS

EXAMPLE

Final Sample Size Desired = 200

Type of Instrument	Percentage Adjustment	Upward Adjust Sample By	Actual Sample Size Needed (for n=200)
Group	10%	20	220
In-Person	10% - 20%	20 - 40	220 - 240
Phone	25%	50	250
Mail	60% - 100%	120 - 200	320 - 400

SUMMARY

Chapter 6 has presented issues concerning common sampling techniques and data collection methods. Sampling methods were described and then presented in a tabular form, indicating the advantages and disadvantages of various methods. Additionally, a discussion of the approaches to sample size determination was presented. Next, data collection methods were described. Advantages and disadvantages of various common data collection techniques were presented in tabular form, together with selection criteria.

The researcher should now be able to decide upon the optimal sampling technique, sample size, and data collection procedures for use in their research endeavor. Suggested readings are also provided. Checklist VI should be fully completed before proceeding to the next chapter.

REFERENCES AND SUGGESTED READINGS

The list below has been selected with the utmost care. The listing has been purposely limited to only those texts which are of a great practical and useful value to most doctoral or professional researchers. Not every entry may be still in print, but generally a search to locate such a book will be very worthwhile. Entries denoted with a double asterisk (**) are those highly recommended for the topic specified. Parenthetical comments for each entry are added by this author.

**Dillman, D. Mail and Telephone Surveys. New York: John Wiley, 1978.

(A unique and very good book concerning strictly mail and phone survey methods—"must" reading for those doing such surveys.)

Kerlinger, F. N. Foundations of Behavioral Research, 2nd ed. New York: Holt, Rinehart and Winston, Inc., 1973.

(As is expected from this text, a good presentation on sampling methods; see pp. 117-133.)

**Sudman, S. Applied Sampling. New York: Academic Press, 1976.

(A unique and practical text on various sampling procedures; a particularly good presentation on stratified and cluster sampling, with easy reading.)

Survey Research Center. Interviewers Manual. Ann Arbor: Institute for Social Research, 1972.

(An interesting small book describing interview techniques, with an additional discussion on cluster sampling.)

CHECKLIST VI

( ) 1. Understand these terms: population, sample, and sample size.

( ) 2. Review the common sampling methods. Do you clearly comprehend the differences between each method?

( ) 3. Carefully consider the <u>Seven Sampling Criteria</u> in terms of your own research project. Complete Worksheet 6.1B using 6.1A as an example. A firm decision on sampling method should be made at this point.

( ) 4. Use the text and Table 6.3 to help select the optimum data collection method for your project.

( ) 5. Determine both initial and final sample sizes utilizing Table 6.4. Use Table 6.5 as an example.

( ) 6. Review the Suggested Readings and comments.

Statistical Analysis   7

INTRODUCTION

    Chapter 7 describes common types of statistical analysis used in doctoral and professional research. Obviously, the topic of statistical analysis is very broad, with multitudes of both simple and complex theories, procedures and formulae. The purpose of this chapter is to present in more concise terms the statistical methods used in most dissertations and, more importantly, their conditions for proper use. This chapter, by no means, constitutes a complete statistical text; there are plenty of those already available! The top texts in the field, relative to doctoral or most professional research needs, are listed in References and Suggested Readings at the chapter's conclusion.

    Throughout the chapter, no assumption of any kind regarding statistical background is made. The presentation is not meant to be a course in mathematical statistics, as the highly technical aspects of statistics and computer analysis are of little concern here. The presentation describes locating, in the most practical sense, the right statistic for the right job. These statistical analysis choices revert back to how one has originally designed the study and, subsequently, the hypotheses. As will be seen, in choosing the right statistical procedure, there really is a method to the madness!

    Why bother using statistical analysis? The study of science and the resulting incremental gains in knowledge are built upon objective investigation and their repeated replication. Statistical analysis provides an objective tool for researchers to use in measuring their findings and comparing them to their previous expectations.

    So what about your study? Regarding both doctoral and professional research, statistical analysis provides an objective and defendable method of analysis subject to accurate replication. In this manner, statistical analysis can test null hypotheses and other related research issues and begin to establish "facts" from enough future replications.

Many times researchers feel that statistical analysis creates undesired complexity within the framework of their project. Oftentimes, the topic of statistical analysis so terrifies a student that its usefulness and value in actually simplifying the research process is not recognized. Such fears will be addressed here.

At this point, a brief review of some fundamental terms and concepts is necessary:

Continuous Data. Data which are comprised of ongoing, varying values are considered continuous data. Among the many examples are number of years at a residence, age, distances, test scores, scaled scores, I.Q.'s, yearly income, height, and weight.

Categorical (or Discrete, Discontinuous) Data. Categorical data are, very simply, forms of data which fall into groupings or divisions. Common examples of categorical data include sex (male/female), political affiliation (Republican/Democrat/Independent/other), blood type (A/B/O), favorite color (blue/green/orange/black), etc.

CONTINUOUS VERSUS
CATEGORICAL DATA

The use of continuous or categorical data has a profound effect on statistical analysis methods available for use. A quick study of the relationships between these data types is mandatory. Note that some information collected as continuous data can be later categorized to form categorical data. However, information originally collected as categorical data can never be later made continuous. As an example, age data originally collected in four age ranges (categories) could never be re-evaluated later as continuous data.

Consider Table 7.1. Notice that when treating data as continuous, more exact information regarding, in this case, respondent age is always yielded. Accurate assessments of mean, range, standard deviation, variance, and other statistics also become possible. If data are

collected as categorical, much detail is forever lost.
No precise assessments of mean or median age, for
example, are now possible. Still referring to Table
7.1, notice that five respondents appear in the "16 or
more years" category, and if this was in fact the
method by which the data were originally collected, the
researcher might not realize that the ages actually
comprising that category went from 16 years old up to
52!

DOCTORAL MORAL VII

Of course, certain variables (e.g., sex, race,
religion) are categorical by nature, but whenever given a choice, <u>always</u> collect data in its
continuous form. Continuous data can be trans-
formed later into categorical data, if desired.
It just doesn't work the other way around!

TABLE 7.1

CONTINUOUS AND CATEGORICAL DATA

CONTINUOUS DATA				CATEGORICAL DATA
Specific Ages		Categorical Ranges		Number per Category
2 3 5	.....	a. 1-5 years old	.....	3
6 8	.....	b. 6-10 years old	.....	2
12 13	.....	c. 11-15 years old	.....	2
16 17 18 35 52	.....	d. 16 or more years old	.....	5

CONTINUOUS DATA		IF TREATED AS		CATEGORICAL DATA
12	=	Number of Respondents (n)	=	12
15.58	=	Mean Age (in years)	=	Don't Know
51 (52-2+1)	=	Age Range	=	Don't Know
14.57	=	Standard Deviation	=	Don't Know
212.28	-	Variance (in years of age)	=	Don't know

124

Note in Table 7.1, continuous data always gives more information about the variable(s) than categorical data does. Further, categorical data can never be changed into continuous data, but continuous data can always be changed into categorical data.

MEASUREMENT SCALES

Data falls into one of four measurement scales: nominal, ordinal, interval, or ratio. Remember the acronym "NOIR" for the correct order, going from the lowest and weakest measurement scale (nominal) to the highest and strongest measurement scale (ratio).

Nominal data, the lowest measurement scale, simply uses numbers (or any symbol) to identify objects, people, places, etc. Nominal data has no intrinsic measure of quantity attached to it. Examples include numbers on racehorses, baseball jersey numbers, or phone numbers. Nominal data is always categorical data.

Ordinal data, as its name implies, simply sets numbers into some rank order. The order can be established as highest to lowest or lowest to highest. An example includes a baseball team's place in the standings (e.g., the author's beloved, and very consistent, fifth place Detroit Tigers). Ordinal data is usually considered categorical data.

Interval data provides a true quantity value on numbers, without regard to a "true zero-point." The best example of interval data is temperature. A measure of 85 degrees is not based on zero degrees being the "total absence of heat," but rather divides up the heat range into intervals (i.e., degrees), without any true zero-point (degrees Kelvin notwithstanding for chemistry majors). Interval data is always continuous data.

Ratio data, the highest measurement scale, again sets a true quantity value on numbers, but now _with_ regard to a true zero-point. On a classroom test of ten questions, a student getting seven correct answers receives a "score" of seven. This score is of the ratio measurement type, since a true zero-point of zero correct does in fact exist and is the fundamental base from which the score of seven is derived. Other common examples of ratio data include age, weight, height, and most test scores. Ratio data is always continuous data. Table 7.2 presents the four measurement scales, with common examples shown for each.

TABLE 7.2

MEASUREMENT SCALES

Measurement Scale Type	Data Form	Purpose and Examples
NOMINAL	CATEGORICAL	TO IDENTIFY *numbers on a racehorse, baseball player's back, phone numbers
ORDINAL	CATEGORICAL (usually)	TO SET IN ORDER BY RANKS *racehorse's finishing place, team's place in standings
INTERVAL	CONTINUOUS	TO SET A VALUE WITHOUT REGARD TO A TRUE ZERO POINT *temperature, I.Q. tests
RATIO	CONTINUOUS	TO SET A VALUE WITH REGARD TO A TRUE ZERO POINT *weight, age, test scores when "0" means "none correct"

One sentence to help remember all four measurement scale types:

"RACEHORSE NUMBER 7 FINISHED IN 3RD PLACE, IN 80 DEGREE HEAT, WITH A TIME OF 2 MINUTES."

Nominal: Racehorse Number 7   (identifies)

Ordinal: finished 3rd   (orders)

Interval: in 80 degree heat   (temperature; no true zero-point)

Ratio: time of 2 minutes   (clocked time; true zero-point at race's start)

DESCRIPTIVE STATISTICS

This form of statistical method concerns merely the description of data found in a study. Examples of descriptive statistics include the mean, mode, median, standard deviation, variance, and response percentages of a particular continuous variable. Oftentimes, graphs and charts are presented with regard to descriptive data to assist in explaining the statistics.

As an example, if 18% of all respondents were 90 years of age, 18% is a descriptive statistic; it describes what proportion of respondents were 90 years old. As a second example, if the mean weight of all respondents was 162 pounds, this is a descriptive statistic; it describes the average weight of respondents. Common types of descriptive statistics, together with their uses, are shown in a concise form within Table 7.3. Review the table at this time.

TABLE 7.3

TYPES AND USES OF DESCRIPTIVE STATISTICS

(COMMONLY USED WITH INTERVAL OR RATIO MEASUREMENT SCALES)

Descriptive Statistic	Symbol	Uses
Counts, Percentages	none	To break down and describe categorical or continuous data in a tabular (frequency distribution) form.
Mean	$\overline{X}$	Accurate measure of average if distribution is reasonably normal. Arithmetic average.
Mode	none	Value(s) or score(s) occurring most often in a distribution.
Median	MDN	Accurate measure of average if distribution is not reasonably normal. One-half of the distribution values are above the median, one-half below.
Standard Deviation	s or σ	Measures dispersion (spread) of scores or values around the mean score or value, in practical terms.

TABLE 7.3 (continued)

Descriptive Statistic	Symbol	Uses
Variance	s^2 or σ^2	Describes dispersion (spread) of scores or values around the mean score or value, in <u>theoretical</u> terms.
Skewness	none	A measure of normality of a distribution in terms of range of scores or values. Right or left curve shift measurement.
Kurtosis	none	A measure of normality of a distribution in terms of frequency of score or value occurrence. Flat or peaked curve measurement.
Standard Error of the Mean	$s_{\bar{x}}$	A measure of statistical accuracy with regard to a mean value from a distribution.
Range	none	Measures entire width of a distribution, from lowest to highest score or value.

TABLE 7.3 (continued)

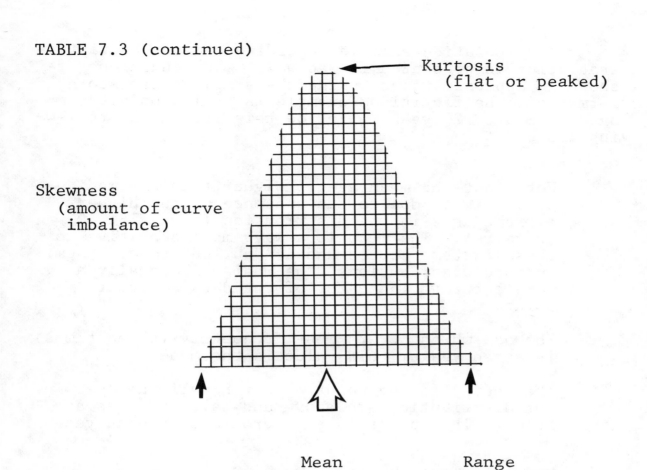

Skewness
   (amount of curve
    imbalance)

Kurtosis
   (flat or peaked)

Mean
Median
Mode

Range
   (between
    horizontal
    dark arrows)

     A standard normal curve, as pictured above,
has the mean, median and mode equal to each other.
The range measures the entire width of the distribution.
The kurtosis measures the flatness or peakedness of the
curve, while the skewness addresses the amount of curve
imbalance between right and left halves of the
distribution.

A calculation example regarding common descriptive statistics is presented in Table 7.4. Calculations are shown in approximations, using the simplest raw score formulae. The fictitious example is of 15 subjects, aged from 5 to 22 years. Follow this listing in reviewing Table 7.4:

1   Note that the mean age is higher than the median age; this is due to the presence of the higher extreme ages in the distribution (e.g., 18, 19, 22 years). The mean is always more sensitive to these extreme scores and is "pulled" toward them. In such distributions, the median is usually a more accurate indicator of the data's center point.

2   The age which occurs most frequently (three times) is seven years; this value is the mode.

3   The median is the point at which half the ages in the distribution are above and half the ages are below. This point is at approximately nine years of age.

4   The standard deviation, derived from an approximate raw score formula, is 5.47. Other descriptive statistics are listed with their formulae.

Note that the example utilizes continuous data (i.e., ages). If data are of the categorical form (e.g., sex, race, religion, marital status, etc.) the frequency distribution table would still provide useful information, however, values for the mean, median, mode, and all other descriptive statistics would become nonsensical. As an example, a categorical variable such as sex of respondents does not have a fluctuating quantity. A male is a male; a female is a female, with no quantity of gender attached to it, this despite what Hollywood keeps trying to tell us!

INFERENTIAL STATISTICS

As researchers wish to test null hypotheses or otherwise make inferences about their data findings to a population, the statistical method of inferential statistics is applied. In this case, the researcher is no longer content to simply describe the findings, but

TABLE 7.4

CALCULATION EXAMPLES OF COMMON

DESCRIPTIVE STATISTICS

Variable: Respondent Age (continuous data; ratio measurement scale)

Number of Subjects: n = 15

Frequency Distribution:

Subject	Age	Subject	Age	Subject	Age
A	5	F	8	K	16
B	6	G	8	L	16
C	7	H	9	M	18
D	7	I	12	N	19
E	7	J	14	O	22

Descriptive Statistic Calculations:
(approximate)

Mean $= \dfrac{\Sigma X}{n} = \dfrac{174}{15} = 11.6$ years of age

Mode $=$ 7 years of age (occurs 3 times)

Median $=$ MDN = 9 years of age (7 ages below, 7 ages above this point)

Standard Deviation $= s = \sqrt{\dfrac{\Sigma X^2}{n} - \overline{X}^2} = 5.47$

Variance $= s^2 = 5.47^2 = 29.97$

Standard Error of the Mean $= \dfrac{s}{\sqrt{n}} = \dfrac{5.47}{\sqrt{15}} = \dfrac{5.47}{3.87} = 1.41$

Range $=$ 5 to 22 (lowest age to highest age)

additionally wants to scientifically test the data and then make objective inferences to a population, of which the sample was presumably representing.

As an example, review a study of career education knowledge in fifth graders. Descriptive data may indicate boy and girl mean scores of 75 and 85, respectively. Note that the descriptive procedure simply describes the boy and girl mean scores. But is this difference between boy and girl scores really a statistically significant difference, or is it simply a chance fluctuation which could perhaps even reverse itself in another similar study? At this point, inferential statistics would be used to test such a question. An inference about the difference found in these sample fifth grade boys and girls will be made about the population of fifth grade boys and girls.

The inferential statistics methods available for the researcher's use are vast and varied, depending upon the type of analysis required and the continuous or categorical forms of the variables being studied.

Parametric and Non-Parametric Statistical Tests—What's the Difference?

At this point, the basic terminology of parametric and non-parametric tests needs to be introduced. An excellent discussion is further provided by Kerlinger (1973). Simply stated, whether the data collected are parametric or non-parametric will determine which forms of inferential statistics are appropriate for the analysis.

PARAMETRIC STATISTICAL TESTS

Parametric statistical tests must use data which satisfy this listing of the Three Critical Parametric Assumptions:

1   The assumption of normality—samples upon which the research is done must be selected from populations which are normally distributed.

2   An assumption of homogeneity of variance—this
means that the spread (i.e., variance or standard
deviation) of dependent variable (i.e., scores) within
the group tested must be statistically equal. This does
not mean that the <u>scores</u> between groups to be tested
need be equal, but that the <u>spread</u> of scores (i.e., the
shape of each group's distributional curve) should be
equal.

3   Parametric statistical methods require that dependent variables (i.e., scores) to be analyzed are
of a continuous form with equal intervals of quantity
measurement. Therefore, categorical dependent variables
cannot be tested by parametric techniques.

If data collected satisfies all three assumptions,
parametric or non-parametric inferential statistical
tests may be used, although parametric procedures are
recommended. If any of the three assumptions are vio-
lated by the data, then non-parametric inferential
statistical tests should be used.

NON-PARAMETRIC STATISTICAL TESTS

Non-parametric statistical tests need none of the
above three parametric assumptions satisfied for their
proper application. Non-parametric statistical tests
can be applied in almost any research situation; they
are fairly easy to understand and are quite simple to
calculate, in most instances. In certain cases, a non-
parametric statistical test might be nicely applied in a
parametric situation, particularly if any parametric
assumptions are in doubt. Usually, the non-parametric
methods serve as the statistical tests for nominal or
ordinal scaled variables.

SELECTING THE PROPER STATISTICAL METHOD

How does the researcher decide which particular
statistical test to use from the many available? <u>Use
this Four-Point Statistics Selection Guide</u>:

1   Determine if a null hypothesis (or some other
unhypothesized issue) is testing for <u>difference</u>
between two or more groups (refer to Table 7.5)
or <u>relationship</u> within one group (refer to Table

7.6). If not testing anything, common inferential statistics are not needed; consult the previous section on descriptive statistics.

2   Determine which variables (i.e., groups and/or scores) are of which scale types (nominal, ordinal, interval, or ratio), within the proper table.

3   For the particular combination of scale types, notice if the test type shown in the table is "P" (i.e., parametric). If it is, review the Three Critical Parametric Assumptions discussed earlier. Ensure that the data meets these assumptions. If not, use a non-parametric ("NP") procedure instead. This is a critical step!

4   Read across the table for the most common and appropriate statistical test, a practical example, and a sample null hypothesis.

Obviously, many other less common statistical approaches can be used, but Tables 7.5, 7.6, and 7.7 provide the appropriate procedures for the vast majority of doctoral dissertations and other professional research. A brief explanatory discussion of both common and other lesser used statistical methods follows.

COMMON PARAMETRIC
STATISTICAL TECHNIQUES

t-Test

The t-test (or Student's t) is the most common and popular statistical test used in, particularly, doctoral research. Very simply, the t-test is used to test for group mean differences when there are two groups. As an example, fifth grade boys and girls could be tested for difference in math aptitude pre-test scores. The t-test can, as such, be used to test two groups on a pre-test only; two groups on a post-test only; one group on pre-test versus post-test; or two groups on gain scores (i.e., post-test minus pre-test scores). A value of "t" is derived with an associated significance (probability) level. Parametric assumptions should be met by the data. There should be a minimum of 30 subjects per group. Computer analysis is recommended, and is usually mandatory if sample size exceeds 50 subjects.

TABLE 7.5

SELECTION GUIDE FOR COMMON STATISTICAL METHODS

Data Type	Statistical Method	Testing For	
		Differences (between groups)	Relationships (within 1 group)
CATEGORICAL [Nominal, Ordinal] → Non-Parametric		Chi-Square	Contingency Coefficient
CONTINUOUS [Interval, Ratio] → Parametric		ANOVA (3+ groups) t-Test (2 groups)	Pearson Correlation Multiple Regression Discriminant Analysis*

*If variable to be predicted is categorical

137

TABLE 7.6

SELECTING THE APPROPRIATE STATISTICAL TEST: FOR DIFFERENCES (2 OR MORE GROUPS)

KEY: N = nominal } categorical data   I = interval } continuous data   NP = non-parametric test
      O = ordinal   R = ratio   P = parametric test

Scores are:	Groups are:	Test Type	Appropriate Statistical Test	Practical Example	Typical Null Hypotheses
N	N	NP	Chi-Square	Political party preference by sex.	There will be no significant difference between men and women regarding their political party preference.
O	N	NP	Mann-Whitney U or Chi-Square	Ranking on English test by student sex.	There will be no significant difference between girls and boys in relation to their ranking on the English test.
O	O	NP	Chi-Square	Grade point average rank by English achievement rank.	There will be no significant difference in grade point average rank as compared to English achievement rank.
I	N	P	If 2 means tested: t-Test If 3 means or more: ANOVA, ANCOVA	Temperature by city.	There will be no significant difference in mean temperature between L.A. and Detroit
R	N	P	If 2 means tested: t-Test If 3 means or more: ANOVA, ANCOVA	Math score by student sex.	There will be no significant difference in math scores between male and female students.
I	-	P	Factor Analysis	To establish 6 factors from a 100-item self-esteem instrument; also to establish construct validity in an instrument.	
R	-	P	Factor Analysis		

138

TABLE 7.7

SELECTING THE APPROPRIATE STATISTICAL TEST: FOR RELATIONSHIPS (1 GROUP)

KEY: N = nominal } categorical data   I = interval } continuous data   NP = non-parametric test
      O = ordinal   R = ratio   P = parametric test

One Variable(s) Scores are:	The Other Variables(s) Scores	Test Type	Appropriate Statistical Test	Practical Example	Typical Null Hypotheses
N	N	NP	Contingency Coefficient	Color preference by sex.	There will be no significant relationship between color preference and sex of respondent.
N	O	NP	Contingency Coefficient or Spearman's rho	Political preference by ranking in education.	There will be no significant relationship between political preference & education.
O	O	NP	Spearman's rho	Math ranking by reading ranking within the 6th grade.	There will be no significant relationship between math ranking and reading ranking within the 6th grade.
O	R	NP or P	Spearman's rho (NP) / Pearson's r (P)	Anxiety scores by self-esteem scores (bi-variate)	There will be no significant relationship between anxiety scores and self-esteem scores.
I	I	P	If 2 variables: Pearson's r / If 3 or more variables: Multiple Regression R	Anxiety scores by self-esteem scores, alienation scores, and IQ scores (multi-variate).	There will be no significant relationship in anxiety scores in regard to self-esteem, alienation, and IQ scores.
I	R	P	" " "		
R	R	P	" " "		
R	N	P	Discriminant Analysis	Income, years in residence, years of schooling, age by respondent sex.	There will be no significant relationship between respondent sex in regard to income, years in residence, years of schooling and age of respondent.
I	N	P	Discriminant Analysis		

Optimum readings for the t-test procedure are Runyan and Haber (1976), and Nie, et al (1981).

Analysis of Variance (ANOVA)

The ANOVA is the most traditionally and widely accepted form of statistical analysis. Again testing for group mean differences, ANOVA can test two or more group means utilizing a single statistical operation. As an example, job satisfaction scores could be tested for difference between three or more occupational groups (e.g., bankers, lawyers, professors). ANOVA accomplishes its statistical testing by comparing variance between the groups to the variance within each group. A resulting F-ratio (variance between divided by variance within) and an associated significance level is found. Parametric assumptions should be met by the data. There should be a minimum of 20 to 30 subjects per group per observation. Computer analysis is required. Numerous volumes have been written regarding many complex ANOVA designs and related procedures for use in almost any research situation. Excellent readings are Senter (1969), and Kerlinger (1973).

Pearson r

The Pearson product-moment linear correlation co-efficient (r), is a very popular parametric statistical measure of relationship between two continuous data variables. Pearson r is used when the researcher wishes to study how a change in one variable may tend to be related to a change in a second variable.

As an example, a Pearson r could be applied to height and weight (continuous) data taken from 40 sample subjects. Note that since Pearson r is a measure of relationship, both the height and weight data must be collected from the identical 40 subjects (i.e., there is only one group of subjects and the data is "paired"). A resulting "r" value and an associated significance (probability) level would assess both the direction (+ or direct; - or inverse) and the strength (between 0 and 1.00) of the relationship between the two variables.

Parametric assumptions should be met by the data. A minimum of 30 subjects, with data on both variables for each subject should be used. Computer analysis is recommended, but not required unless sample size exceeds roughly 50.

Interpretation of correlations should be done cautiously. First, a large sample size can easily produce a statistically significant r value, but still with very little actual strength of relationship between the variables. Secondly, correlation is not causation. This point warrants another doctoral moral, as follows:

DOCTORAL MORAL VIII

Because two variables are significantly related they do not necessarily cause each other to vary.

As an example, player height and points scored in basketball may be significantly and positively correlated (i.e., taller players score more points), but a player scoring thousands of points won't grow an inch due to playing ability!

Suggested readings regarding Pearson correlation are Runyan and Haber (1976), and Nie, et al (1981).

Multiple Regression, R

Similar to the bivariate (two variable) Pearson r, multiple regression studies relationships between one dependent measure and two or more independent measures, all using continuous data. Thus, it is a "multivariate" statistical technique. As an example, multiple regression could be used to evaluate the relationship between one variable, perhaps self-esteem, and two or more other variables, perhaps alienation and anxiety. The analysis would assess the correlation of alienation and anxiety considered simultaneously in relation to self-esteem.

This technique represents a powerful, practical and realistic approach to many research situations, particularly in the behavioral sciences. Parametric assumptions should be met by the data. A minimum of 50 subjects, with all scores on all subjects, is recommended for use with this procedure. Computer analysis is mandatory. The identical interpretation warnings as discussed for Pearson r correlation above would also apply for this procedure.

Multiple regression can become very complex as the number of variables under analysis increases. Many texts are available on the subject; some are simple and practical, but most are complex and quite theoretical. The selected references representing the former type of presentation style are Nie, et al (1981), and Kerlinger (1973).

Discriminant Analysis

This somewhat popular multivariate statistical procedure involves the use of one categorical dependent variable (i.e., groups) as related to numerous continuous independent variables (i.e., scores). Discriminant analysis represents, in a sense, a multiple regression analysis but with a categorical instead of continuous dependent variable.

Considering the same example just used for multiple regression, if the self-esteem data were simply collected as categorical data (e.g., high, medium, low self-esteem) instead of continuous score data, then discriminant analysis could be used to assess the relationships of alienation and anxiety in reference to these categorical levels of self-esteem.

Parametric assumptions should be met by the data. A minimum of 50 subjects, with full data on each, is recommended for use with this procedure. The identical interpretation warnings as discussed for Pearson r correlation would also apply. Discriminant analysis can become very complex as the number of variables increase. Computer analysis is mandatory.

Naturally, as in the case of all multivariate techniques, the utility and power of discriminant analysis is very wide, and is obviously only summarized here. The best texts are Nie, et al (1981), and Bennett and Bowers (1976) for the least mathematically intimidating presentations.

Factor Analysis

Developed mainly through the field of psychology, factor analysis is a powerful data reduction technique also belonging to the family of multivariate, parametric statistics. As an example, in a 200-question test instrument assessing job satisfaction, factor analysis might be used to reduce the 200 questions to perhaps 10 factors (or constructs). Each factor would represent a specific aspect of job satisfaction, as measured by the instrument. Certain of the 200 questions would strongly relate to one particular factor, while other questions would relate more strongly to other factors. Factors could be autonomous or overlapping, depending upon the type of factor analysis "rotation" applied.

Additionally, since factor analysis is used to determine and evaluate factors within test instruments, it serves as a tool for use in test item revision or in establishing construct validity (see Chapter V). The computations behind such processes are complex. Different factor analysis techniques are available for use, with selection dependent upon the type of research situation and theoretical framework of the study.

Intrinsically, factor analysis also contains within it elements of subjective judgment on the part of the researcher. This is viewed by some academics and other professionals as a positive aspect of the method, while others feel that factor analysis is not strictly scientific, due to this subjective aspect.

If using factor analysis, parametric assumptions should be met by the data. Minimum sample size should be quite large, usually about six to ten times the number of instrument questions (e.g., to factor analyze a 50-item instrument, sample a minimum of 300 to 500 subjects). This sampling formula is simply a rough guide; individual research topics and varied instrument complexities can alter the minimum sampling quantity considerably. All factor analysis requires a computer.

Numerous texts are available concerning factor analysis but, unfortunately, nearly all are difficult to understand for non-mathematically inclined doctoral or professional researchers. It is mandatory that those interested in utilizing factor analytic methods first consult with their advisors and, second, read all the optimum suggested readings before instrument development and data collection phases occur. The readings highlighted below are clearly the most practical and readable texts to date: Bennett and Bowers (1976), Kerlinger (1973), and Nie, et al (1981).

COMMON NON-PARAMETRIC STATISTICS

Chi-Square (χ^2)

The most popular of all non-parametric inferential statistical methods is chi-square (pronounced: kī-square). Chi-square tests for differences between categorical variables (i.e., nominal or ordinal data). There are both "one-way" and "two-way" chi-square procedures.

As an example of a one-way chi-square analysis, consider asking a sample group of subjects one question regarding the political party they prefer, assuming the question on the instrument form requires a categorical (e.g., Democratic, Republican, Independent, etc.) response. The one-way chi-square would test for differences in popularity between the political party categories, relative to the sample's responses to the question.

A two-way chi-square is used if two categorical variables are to be compared. If the sample group discussed above were split into male and female, thus creating a new variable, "sex of respondent," then this categorical variable could be compared (or "cross-tabulated") to political party choice. In this way, comparisons between the sexes on political party preference may be evaluated (e.g., significantly more males are Republican and more females are Democrat).

Both the one-way and two-way chi-square procedures result in a chi-square value and associated significance (probability) level. Chi-square is a non-parametric statistic and, as such, requires no parametric data assumptions. The data must be categorical in nature. The statistical procedure is quite simple and, for samples under 50, or when a small number of chi-square analyses are to be calculated, a computer is usually not required. Larger studies with either greater sample sizes or numerous chi-square tests planned should be computer analyzed. Recommended reading regarding chi-square is Siegal (1953).

Spearman's rho (r_s)

Spearman's rho (pronounced: rō) is a measure of relationship (i.e., correlation) between two variables, each scored in terms of ranks (i.e., ordinal data). As an example, a classroom of students could be ranked on both math and science skills. If a strong relationship

144

exists within the students in these two skills, the
Spearman rho correlation coefficient between the rankings will be high (i.e., near +1.00)(see Siegel, 1953).

The Spearman procedure will result in a coefficient value and associated significance (probability)
level. Since the procedure is non-parametric, no
assumptions need be met by the data, other than the
variable scores be in ranked form and that data are
collected for each respondent on each score. In studies
with sample sizes under 50 and minimal numbers of correlation calculations required, a computer is not needed.

Contingency Coefficient (C)

This non-parametric statistic is also a measure of
relationship. It is used when one or both variables
under investigation are of a nominal form, rather than
in a ranked order. Data is collected, categorized and
placed into a two-way table for analysis.

As an example, a contingency coefficient could
test for a significant relationship between years of
residence in a community and family income level, for
any given sample. One or both of the variables could
be in the form of categorical data. Additionally, no
tedious or time-consuming rankings are needed.

The contingency coefficient has its limitations,
however. The coefficient's significance level ever-
changes as a function of the specific cell dimensions in
the two-way table; this makes it impossible to directly
compare this statistic to a Pearson r or Spearman rho.
Nonetheless, in a wide range of research situations, it
provides a good measure of relationship in a non-
parametric situation (refer to Siegal, 1953).

NULL HYPOTHESES, STATISTICAL SIGNIFICANCE, AND ALPHA LEVELS

All statistical measures yield a significance
(common synonym: probability) value. This value always
relates to the hypothesis of no difference or no relationship (i.e., the null hypothesis). More specifically, the significance value associated with any
statistical test actually represents the odds of the
results being due only to chance, and not due to any
real difference or relationship found in the data.

145

As an example, in a study of boys' and girls' math scores, a t-test value which yields a significance value of .04 indicates that the boy and girl groups under study would have different group mean scores due to chance only 4% of the time. Conversely, 96% of the time the mean difference in math scores between the boy and girl groups must be not due to chance; thus, the difference must be due to other factors (e.g., sex of student).

As a second example, a researcher using a two-way chi-square may find a significance value of .02 in a study of political party affiliation as related to respondent sex. In this case, a difference in political party affiliation in relation to respondent sex would be due to chance only 2% of the time. Conversely, 98% of the time the differences found in political party affiliation would not be due to chance; they must be due to other factors (i.e., sex of respondent).

The significance value obtained answers the question: What are the chances that the null hypothesis (i.e., the statement of no difference or no relationship) is true? Granted, the concept of the null hypothesis as it relates to statistical testing can be confusing. Re-read the moral as needed. It will come to you!

DOCTORAL MORAL IX

As the significance value found goes <u>down</u>, the chances of the null hypothesis being true goes <u>down</u> and, hence, the chances of a real difference or relationship existing in the data goes <u>up</u>.

At what level is the significance value considered a "significant finding" in testing null hypotheses? The level selected as the statistical testing criteria or "cut-off" is termed the "alpha level." The .05 and .01 alpha levels are by far the most traditionally accepted in most research work. Simply stated, the alpha level represents the percentage chance of being wrong, if null is rejected.

At the .05 alpha level, the researcher is willing to reject the null hypothesis (the idea of no difference or relationship) if the significance value found by the appropriate statistical test is .05 or less. As an example, if a significance value of .03 were found from a statistical test, the null hypothesis would be rejected at an alpha level of .05. There would be only a 3% chance of being wrong in rejecting null. The researcher would conclude there probably is a real difference or relationship in the data.

The next issue relates to how and when to select an alpha level. First, it is important to understand that if alpha is set too high (e.g., .10) many statistical tests can yield "significant" findings, but rejecting the null hypothesis when, in fact, it really is true, may result. Second, if alpha is set too low (e.g., .001) a true significant finding may not be recognized, since it is not good enough to be statistically significant. When setting an alpha level, determine what the consequences are of being wrong in the statistical decision. Severe consequences will dictate a lower alpha level (e.g., .01, .001). In many cases, either advisors or previous research precedent will dictate the alpha level(s); just be sure the reasoning behind the alpha level selected is understood and can be defended. Usually, one alpha level is used throughout a study, but varying them for each hypothesis is acceptable, as long as suitable rationale is provided.

The alpha level(s) should always be set before the study begins. It is improper to alter alpha either during the study or, even worse!—after witnessing the statistical test results. Students usually feel that their study must yield statistically significant findings. In answer to this thinking, the following moral is presented:

DOCTORAL MORAL X

In a soundly designed study, the true worth of the research has nothing to do with whether or not statistically significant outcomes were found. Finding no statistically significant results can be very "significant," depending upon the interpretation of the results.

> *"There are three kinds of lies:*
>
> *lies,*
> *damn lies,*
> *and statistics."*
>
> —Disraeli (1804-1881)

It is entirely possible to lie with statistics, as perhaps everyone who ever watched television commercials or read a magazine advertisement well knows. What Disraeli didn't mention was that one cannot only lie with statistics, but can also greatly "bend" the truth! See Huff (1954) for an amusing short text.

In doctoral dissertations or other professional research, it is not advisable to either lie or bend the truth with statistics. It is just simply not worth it. No matter how good the project is, all research work has limitations, shortcomings, and design errors of some magnitude; all of which can be described and subsequently improved upon. Do not falsify data or analytical results; it is a very dangerous and inappropriate practice.

Lecture: The ultimate goal of the scientific method is to achieve truth through objective analysis and replication. It is impossible for deceit to lead to the goal of ultimate truth. A study using false results or terrible design is totally in opposition to the exact scientific theory which the study is itself representing.

DOCTORAL MORAL XI

Doing no study is better than doing an unethical one.

SUMMARY

Chapter 7 has summarized statistical terminology, including descriptive and inferential statistics, types of measurement scales, continuous/categorical data forms, and common parametric/non-parametric types of statistical tests. In subject matter of such complexity, the reader is strongly advised to re-read the sections, as needed.

The vast majority of doctoral or professional research work will utilize the methods and statistical tests described, but the information is by no means exhaustive. Further detail regarding statistical testing methods may be found in References and Suggested Readings at this chapter's conclusion.

A Checklist is provided and should be completed before continuing to the next chapter.

REFERENCES AND SUGGESTED READINGS

The list below has been selected with the utmost care. The listing has been purposely limited to only those texts which are of a great practical and useful value to most doctoral or professional researchers. Not every entry may be still in print, but generally a search to locate such a book will be very worthwhile. Entries denoted with a double asterisk (**) are those highly recommended for the topic specified. Parenthetical comments for each entry are added by this author.

**Bennett, S. and Bowers, D. An Introduction to Multi-variate Techniques for Social and Behavioral Sciences. New York: John Wiley, 1976.

("Must" reading for those doing studies involving particularly factor analysis. See pp. 8-55. The presentation is the simplest and clearest text available for the non-statistically oriented.)

Chase, C. Measurement for Education Evaluation, 2nd ed. Reading: Addison-Wesley, 1978.

(A good general purpose text covering fundamentals.)

Dayton, C. The Design of Educational Experiments. New York: McGraw-Hill, 1970.

(A very worthwhile text on analysis of variance procedures provided the reader has a prior background in statistical analysis and block designs.)

Elzey, F. F. A First Reader in Statistics, 2nd ed. Monterey, California: Brooks/Cole Publishing Company, 1974.

(A small text introducing statistics to inexperienced students.)

Huff, D. How to Lie with Statistics. New York: Norton, 1954.

(A very amusing little book, but don't use the methods demonstrated!)

**Kerlinger, F. N. Foundations of Behavioral Research, 2nd ed. New York: Holt, Rinehart and Winston, Inc., 1973.

("Must" reading for those using analysis of variance, multiple regression, or factor analysis. Discussions are characterized by very clear presentations of complex statistical concepts.)

Linton, M., Gallo, P. S., Logan, C. A. The Practical Statistician. Monterey, California: Brooks/Cole Publishing Company, 1975.

(A guidebook approach to using statistical techniques.)

**Lyman, H. B. Test Scores and What They Mean, 3rd ed. Englewood Cliffs, N.J.: Prentice-Hall, Inc., 1978.

(A concise book on test score interpretation; very well done.)

McNeil, K., Kelly, F., and McNeil, J. Testing Research Hypotheses Using Multiple Linear Regression. Southern Illinois University Press, 1975.

(A very good text for those with some statistical and computer experience.)

Minium, E. Statistical Reasoning in Psychology and Education, 2nd ed. New York: John Wiley, 1978.

(A good general purpose text.)

**Nie, N., Hull, C., Jenkins, J., Steinbrenner, K. and Bent, D. Statistical Package for the Social Sciences, combined ed. New York: McGraw-Hill, 1981.

(Designed as a guide to the SPSS computer package, this book is an amazingly good textbook as well. Strong points include discussions on t-tests, Pearson correlation, analysis of variance, factor analysis, and discriminant analysis.)

Runyon, R., and Haber, A. Fundamentals of Behavioral Statistics, 3rd ed., Reading: Addison-Wesley, 1976.

(A good general purpose volume.)

**Senter, R. J. <u>Analysis of Data</u>. Glenview, Illinois: Scott, Foresman and Company, 1969.

(A very good text on overall introductory statistics. Particularly fine presentation on analysis of variance; see pp. 241-293.)

**Siegal, S. <u>Nonparametric Statistics</u>. New York: McGraw-Hill, 1956.

(The classic book of non-parametric statistical methods. Easy reading in a logical format presentation.)

Thorndike, R., and Hagan, E. <u>Measurement and Evaluation in Psychology and Education</u>, 4th ed. New York: Wiley, 1969.

(Good introductory discussion of measurement and related issues.)

CHECKLIST VII

( ) 1. Understand the difference between continuous data and categorical data. Explain it to someone as a self-test. Refer to Table 7.1.

( ) 2. Review the four measurement scales: nominal, ordinal, interval, and ratio. Identify which of your variables are of which scale. Review Table 7.2.

( ) 3. Concerning your comprehension of descriptive statistics, review Tables 7.3 and 7.4 and the accompanying text.

( ) 4. Know the difference between descriptive and inferential statistics. Explain it to someone in one minute.

( ) 5. Use Tables 7.5, 7.6, and 7.7 together with the Four-Step Statistics Selection Guide to choose the appropriate procedure for each test needed. Confirm your choice(s) with your advisor.

( ) 6. For general understanding, review the brief explanations for the more common statistical procedures.

( ) 7. Understand alpha levels; their purpose, and how and when to set them.

( ) 8. Realize that the value of your study does not depend on the statistical significance of your findings.

( ) 9. Review the Suggested Readings and comments.

Overview of Computer Room

High Speed Printer

Practical Computer Use

INTRODUCTION

After establishing the design, instrument, sampling, and statistical analysis to be used in the research work, the next logical concern is computer use. In discussing this issue, included are topics of computer-compatible instruments, data editing, coding, and key-punching. After these sequential steps, developing computer programs to analyze the data is required. Lastly, a structured method by which to analyze sometimes voluminous computer print-outs is presented. Chapter 8 will address all of these topics with the aid of numerous tables and practical examples. The presentation assumes little or no prior exposure to computerized statistical analysis by the reader.

COMPUTER COMPATIBILITY OF INSTRUMENTS AND DATA INPUT METHODS

After arriving at a final instrument form (refer to Chapter V), computer compatibility of the document should be ensured if the project will involve computerized statistical analysis. Making the instrument computer compatible will save time and money in data entry operations and will also reduce data entry errors.

A standard computer card length is 80 columns. Each data card is called a record. Very simply, that means that 80 digits will fit onto one card (record), with one digit per card column. Sometimes numerous cards for each respondent will be needed for longer instruments. <u>Making a published or original instrument computer-compatible involves deciding which data goes into which columns on the card(s)</u>.

Developing computer compatibility in instruments involves two steps:

1   Decide how the responses to each question are to be identified or coded.

2   Decide where these coded responses are to appear
on the computer card(s). It is imperative that
all data be recorded in exactly the identical
order on all data cards, for all respondents. The
computer must know precisely where each piece of
data is for every question on the instrument.
This ordering of data on the computer card is
known as the input format.

In Table 8.1 a simplified example of a computer-
compatible instrument is shown. The item numbers appear
at the far left. The data is entered in spaces or areas
provided. The respondent (or interviewer) is required
to only fill in or circle responses directly onto the
instrument. The numbers in parentheses indicate the
computer card column numbers in which the data will be
keypunched. The example shown has data up to column 11
of a computer card.

In many cases, keypunch personnel can be given
copies of the actual original instruments and data responses can be entered onto cards, tape, or directly
onto a computer disk (more about this later).

In cases where an extremely complex instrument is
not computer compatible and/or large amounts of data
editing (i.e., correcting, recoding, etc.) are needed,
it is much safer and more accurate to transfer responses
from the instruments onto a standard coding form, available from most college bookstores. It is strongly
recommended that only the researcher or others close to
the study be used as the labor force in this data transfer step. Ultimately, the computer will only analyze
what is on the coding forms, and not what is actually on
the original instruments.

Remember, too, in the data coding procedure, to
"clean" the data; that is, remove illegal responses,
decipher hard to discern responses, and recode answers
as necessary. Data transferred to the coding form must
be in precise column locations and very legible. Always
double-check the completed coding forms for accuracy.

Upon completion, coding form copies should be used
by keypunching personnel to keypunch the data. The
original coding forms and original completed instruments
should always be retained by the researcher. No exceptions, ever!

Disk Storage Units

Disk

TABLE 8.1

COMPUTER-COMPATIBLE INSTRUMENT

SIMPLIFIED EXAMPLE

		Data	(Column Numbers)
1.	Respondent ID number	7 3 3 2	(1-4)
2.	Sex (male=1/female=2)	1	(5)
3.	Age in years	2 6	(6-7)

Answer each of the following three items from 1/strongly disagree, to 6/strongly agree. Circle only one number response per item:

		SD	D	d	a	A	SA	
4.	I love statistics.	1	2	3	(4)	5	6	(8)
5.	I enjoy doctoral dissertations.	1	2	3	4	(5)	6	(9)
6.	I must be out of my mind.	1	2	3	4	5	(6)	(10)

7. Highest level of schooling completed (circle one):   4   (11)

        1. grade school
        2. high school
        3. B.A.
        4. M.A.
        5. Ed.D.
        6. Ph.D.
        7. Other _____

8., etc. up to 80 columns, then start second record as needed.

TABLE 8.2

CODING FORM USING DATA RESPONSES FROM TABLE 8.1

A final word of caution: editing, correcting or transferring data onto coding forms can be monotonous operations for enthusiastic researchers. After all, it is only a "clerical task," isn't it? Beware! A mistake here due to impatience or just some old-fashioned day-dreaming can produce disaster later. Please be careful on this clerical, although critical, step.

As an example, Table 8.2 demonstrates how given responses from the instrument shown in Table 8.1 are entered into the correct column positions on a standard coding form. Note how the small column numbers across the top of the coding form correspond with the column numbers in parentheses on the original instrument. Each horizontal line on the standard coding form represents one computer card after the data is punched.

Table 8.3 illustrates a keypunched computer card of the data shown on the coding form in Table 8.2. On most keypunch equipment, the data responses should appear printed across the top of the card. The card column numbers, usually up to 80 columns wide, appear across the card as well. The keypunched cards will be later run through a card reader and will be simultaneously stored on a "disk" for recall by the computer when needed.

The example shown has required less than 80 columns per respondent. If more than 80 columns per respondent were required, a second card, starting in column one, would begin. In cases of multiple cards per respondent, always keypunch respondent identification numbers and the card numbers in the same columns on each card, and keep all the cards in order. As an example, if there are five cards per respondent, all five cards must follow each other in order for that first respondent. Following the first respondent, there must be five cards, in order, for the second respondent, etc. Table 8.4 illustrates data responses in such a situation utilizing five cards (or records) per respondent. Table 8.5 demonstrates the respective transferring of the data onto the standard coding form. Note how a space is left between different respondents' first cards on the coding form, to promote clarity and accuracy for keypunching.

DATA INPUT AND STORAGE METHODS

The examples thus far have described computer cards as the medium for data input (into disk storage) in a computer system, but other data input methods are

TABLE 8.3

COMPUTER CARD DIAGRAM USING TABLE 8.2 CODING FORM

Data printed across top card columns

Holes punched into card field

Card columns

TABLE 8.4

MULTIPLE CARDS (RECORDS) PER RESPONDENT

Respondent No. 1

Card	ID #	Response Codes (Data)	Card # (Record)
1	1111	177781283	1
2	1111	177374893	2
3	1111	168773219	3
4	1111	143441873	4
5	1111	188881777	5

Respondent No. 2

1	1221	155555555	1
2	1221	163211731	2
3	1221	197732101	3
4	1221	114833444	4
5	1221	122158798	5

Card Columns:

    1234   123456789........up to..........80

Card Order for Multiple Card Formats

Example of five cards (records) per case; each line across represents one computer card, 80 columns wide. See Table 8.5 for respective coding form.

TABLE 8.5

CODING FORM USING DATA RESPONSES FROM TABLE 8.4

STATEMENT NUMBER	CONT	FORTRAN STATEMENT	LINE NUMBER
1 1 1 1		7 7 7 8 1 2 6 3	1
1 1 1 1		7 7 3 7 4 8 9 3	2
1 1 1 1		6 8 7 7 3 2 1 9	3
1 1 1 1		9 3 4 4 1 8 7 3	4
1 1 1 1		8 8 8 8 1 7 7 7	5
1 2 2 1		5 5 5 5 5 5 5 5	1
1 2 2 1		6 3 2 1 1 7 3 1	2
1 2 2 1		1 9 7 7 3 2 1 0 1	3
1 2 2 1		1 4 6 3 3 9 4 4	4
1 2 2 1		2 1 5 8 7 9 8	5

also available. Second to computer cards in popularity is computer tape. In this case, data is keypunched (or actually key-entered, since nothing is physically punched) onto a magnetic recording tape. This method is good if the volume of records (not necessarily respondents) is high. Tape will store data much more conveniently than cards and does not require disk storage space in the computer system, as card input always does.

Recommendation: Inexperienced researchers should use cards as long as the number of records does not exceed approximately 2,000. If using tape, consult with someone familiar with your computer center's tape drive equipment for specific details.

At a few very modern installations, the keypunch personnel enter the data from copies of the original instruments or coding forms directly into disk storage within the computer system. Thus, no cards or tape are ever used. This is a convenient data input method worthy of investigation.

Finally, it is possible at some computer installations to use mark-sensitive scan sheets for data input. Each respondent will pencil-in their response in the appropriate spot on a specially designed answer sheet. Later, at high efficiency and low cost, the scan sheets can be read into a computer system and stored on disk or tape. This is a convenient data input method if your instrument(s) can be made compatible with the limitations of scan-sheets. This data input method is worthy of further investigation, particularly if the study will involve many respondents, questions, or both.

No matter what the data input medium, the computer must have a way to access the information for later analysis. Importantly, once data are on disk or tape, it can be easily transferred by computer to any other media as desired. For example, if data are keypunched onto cards, entered into the computer by the card reader and stored on disk, it can easily be copied and transferred to tape. Likewise, additional card decks can be punched by computer from the disk storage; or data on tape can be transferred easily to disk. These procedures are all very quick to implement at most installations. Simply obtain consulting assistance from the particular computer center, as needed.

DATA DICTIONARY

Researchers need a simple and accurate method of knowing where data are stored both by column and record numbers. The Data Dictionary is extremely useful in this regard. Table 8.7 gives an example of the Data Dictionary using the instrument shown in Table 8.6. Follow the Data Dictionary Eight-Step List in studying the two tables:

1   The instrument name is listed in the upper left box of Table 8.7.

2   Each item of information from the instrument is given a variable number; this includes respondent case numbers and all questions (Table 8.6). Instead of using fancy computerized labels to name variables, it's easier to simply start with "V1" for "variable one" and continue. In the example instrument, V1 is the respondent identification number. Likewise, V2 is question number 1, V3 is question number 2, and onward to the final variable, V27. Note that question numbers and variable numbers do not necessarily have to match; in fact, they rarely do, particularly if respondent idenfification numbers or other information (experimental/ control group I.D., etc.) precede the instrument's actual questions or items.

3   In Table 8.7, the card (record) number in which the variable is located is shown, followed by the exact column numbers within the card where the variable's data resides for each respondent. If the variable is numerical, an "F" will appear in the next column; a letter-coded variable is indicated with an "A" in this column.

4   Continuing across in Table 8.7, the computer format is displayed. The symbol "F1.0" would indicate a numerical variable (F) of column width 1, with 0 places behind the decimal point (e.g., 5.). Similarly, the symbol F3.0 would indicate the numerical variable (F) of column width 3, with 0 places behind the decimal point (e.g., 217.). Letter coded variables would have formats such as A1, meaning a letter variable one column wide. (e.g., D). Likewise, A3 would indicate a letter variable three columns wide (e.g., ABF).

165

5   Proceeding across Table 8.7, the measurement scale
        is to be included using symbols N (nominal), O
(ordinal), I (interval), R (ratio). As discussed in
Chapter VIII, the measurement scale can be critically
important in determining the appropriate statistical
tests to be later performed on each variable.

6   The response levels possible for each variable are
        next entered in Table 8.7. If a multiple choice
item has five possible answers, then five "response
levels" are conceivable. If respondent age is asked of
a sample group aged 20 to 60, there are 41 possible
response levels, one for each age.

7   Finally in Table 8.7, a description of each vari-
        able follows, together with a "comments" section
for notes.

8   Make copies of Worksheet 8.7 and complete the Data
        Dictionary for your research study. Fill it out
completely for all variables. The Data Dictionary, when
completed, will help enormously in organizing, programming and analyzing the data.

SUGGESTED COMPUTER
PROGRAMS WITH EXAMPLES

        Before getting involved with actual programming
for statistical analysis of the data, it is always a
good idea to simply list the data file on a computer
print-out. Very simply, the computer will "read" the
data file from disk or tape and "write" what it "sees,"
using one line across the page per record. Using this
line file print-out of the data, make random checks on
the data for correct column and record locations. Why
bother? Because it is entirely possible for a computer
program to run "correctly" but yield incorrect findings
if the data is consistently in the wrong spot within the
data file. A review of the data on a print-out produced
directly from the computer can eliminate a potential
disaster.

        After it is assured that the data resides correctly
on disk or tape, a "control" file or program must be
developed to statistically describe and analyze the data.
What should the researcher generally want in the control

Computer Program Documentation
Volumes

Tape Drive Unit

TABLE 8.6

COMPUTER COMPATIBLE INSTRUMENT FOR USE WITH THE DATA DICTIONARY EXAMPLE FOLLOWING

COMPLEX EXAMPLE

(V1)   ID No: $\frac{3}{(1)}$ $\frac{6}{}$ $\frac{9}{}$ $\frac{5}{}$ $\frac{4}{}$ $\frac{4}{(6)}$

PARENTS, CHILDREN, AND FAMILIES

PART A

Please choose one answer for each of the following four items:

1. When <u>my</u> child has a problem, <u>my</u> most common response is to: (Check one)

    ___ A.   suggest alternatives to the child.

    ___ B.   seek assistance of others.

    ___ C.   listen to the child.

    ___ D.   ignore the problem.   (V2)   (7)

    ___ E.   tell the child to work it out.

    ___ F.   try to solve the problem for the child.

2. When <u>my</u> child bothers me, <u>my</u> most common response is to: (Check one)

    ___ A.   threaten to punish unless the child stops.

    ___ B.   ignore the child.

    ___ C.   leave the room.

    ___ D.   tell child to stop.

    ___ E.   say how it makes me feel.   (V3)   (8)

    ___ F.   tell child why I think child is misbehaving.

    ___ G.   offer a reward for child to change.

    ___ H.   call a third party to decide.

    ___ I.   go to someone for advice.

168

TABLE 8.6 (continued)

3. When there is a conflict between <u>my</u> child and my-self, <u>my</u> most common response is to: (Check one)

   ___ A. be fair but firm in resolving it.

   ___ B. go along with what the child wants.

   ___ C. minimize the difference between us.

   ___ D. use humor to lessen the conflict.

   ___ E. bring in someone else to moderate.

   ___ F. bring in someone else to decide
        what to do.   (V4)   (9)

   ___ G. explain how the child's behavior
        is wrong.

   ___ H. seek a solution acceptable to both.

   ___ I. offer a reward for child to change.

   ___ J. threaten to punish unless the child
        changes.

   ___ K. try to persuade the child through
        reason.

4. When <u>my</u> child has an attitude or opinion of which I don't approve, <u>my</u> most common response is to:
(Check one)

   ___ A. ignore it.

   ___ B. try to persuade the child through
        reason.

   ___ C. send the child to an authority for
        advice.

   ___ D. explore alternative with the child.

   ___ E. threaten to punish unless the child
        changes.   (V5)   (10)

   ___ F. discipline the child.

   ___ G. pretend it doesn't bother me.

   ___ H. support the child's position even
        though I disagree.

   ___ I. argue with the child.

   ___ J. offer a reward for the child to
        change.

TABLE 8.6 (continued)

PART B

In this section of the survey we are concerned with
your attitude and opinions. Below you will find a number of statements regarding parents and children.
Please indicate your agreement or disagreement with
each statement in the following manner:

    Strongly Agree   --   Cross out letter "A"
    Agree   --   Cross out letter "a"
    Undecided   --   Cross out letter "u"
    Disagree   --   Cross out letter "d"
    Strongly Disagree   --   Cross out letter "D"

    For example: If you strongly agree with the
    following statement, you should mark it in this
    way:

    Boys are more active than girls ...... ✗ a u d D

There are no "right" or "wrong" answers. Work just as
rapidly as you can—it is your first impression that we
are interested in.
----

1. Parents have to sacrifice
    everything for their
    children .... A a u d D   (V6) (11)

2. Most of the time, giving
    advice to children is a
    waste of time, because
    they can't take it or
    don't need it .... A a u d D   (V7) (12)

3. It is hard to let children
    go and visit people because
    they might misbehave when
    parents aren't around ..... A a u d D   (V8) (13)

4. A child should be allowed
    to try out what it can do
    at times without parents
    watching .... A a u d D   (V9) (14)

5. It's hard to know what to
    do when a child is afraid . A a u d D   (V10) (15)

TABLE 8.6 (continued)

6. Children shouldn't be asked to do all the compromising without a chance to express their side of things ...... A a u d D   (V11) (17)

7. Children should be seen and not heard .... A a u d D   (V12) (18)

8. It's important to be consistent in reprimanding children .... A a u d D   (V13) (19)

9. The way a child behaves is a direct reflection of his/her parents' attitudes. A a u d D   (V14) (20)

10. No one can really understand a child except another child .... A a u d D   (V15) (21)

TABLE 8.7

THE DATA DICTIONARY

Instrument:
Shown in Table 8.6

Variable (V) Number	Question/Item (Q) Number	Card (Record) Number	Column No's Used	Numerical (F) or Ltr (A)	Format	Measurement Scale	Response Levels Possible	Description	Comments
V1	ID	1	1-6	F	F6.0	N	999,999	Respondent ID number	
V2	Part A/Q1	1	7	A	A1	N	6	When my child has a problem, my most common response is to:	
. . .									
V11	Part B/Q6	1	16	F	F1.0	I	5	Children shouldn't be asked to do ...	Keypunch numerals 1-5 for letters A through D
. . .									
V27	Part B/Q23 (not shown)	1	33	F	F1.0	I	5	Raising children is a nerve-wracking job.	Keypunch numerals 1-5 for letters A through D
. . .									

172

WORKSHEET 8.7

THE DATA DICTIONARY

Instrument: _____

Variable (V) Number	Question/Item (Q) Number	Card (Record) Number	Column No's Used	Numerical (F) or Ltr (A)	Format	Measurement Scale	Response Levels Possible	Description	Comments

file program? This four-point list concisely outlines
the Recommended Programming Sequence:

1   Control Commands. The number of variables and
       input format (the structure of the data file) must
be referenced early in the program. Worksheet 8.7 has
already helped in this regard. Various other control
phrases must also be included, such as: number of
cases (respondents), type of storage used for the data
file, missing values, and variable labels for better
readability on the print-outs.

2   Frequencies Count Command. As far as the analyti-
       cal elements of the program are concerned, the
next set of commands should always call for a frequency
distribution of all variables in the study (refer to
Table 7.5 for a review). This analytical process will
give the researcher a chance to double-check all responses, while looking for obvious mis-punches or other
improper answers to each item on the instrument. Additionally, for interval or ratio (i.e., continuous)
variables, all descriptive statistics (e.g., mean,
median, mode, standard deviation, etc.) should be generated at this same time.

3   Statistical Test Commands for Hypotheses. In
       their original and sequential order, all null
hypotheses in the project should be tested with the
appropriate statistical test. This will involve using
inferential statistical tests, such as t-tests, chi-
square, analysis of variance, or other types of analytical methods previously discussed (refer to Tables 7.5
and 7.6).

4   Statistical Test Commands for Non-Hypotheses.
       Following null hypothesis testing, the computer
program should address unhypothesized findings including
descriptive statistics and inferential statistical tests,
depending on what is desired.

       Of course, transforming variables into other forms
(e.g., changing respondent age from a continuous variable
to a categorical "age-bracketed" variable) can be easily
accomplished by most computers at any time during the
program.

The electromagnetic and mathematical processes which perform these many data manipulations are awesome. Without the computer as a sophisticated tool, researchers would be still in the dark ages of analytical methodology. Modern computer science, which gave us the analytical power and accompanying complications in the first place, has, happily, also presented us with the solution to our potentially complex programming woes!

Today, the extreme sophistication of packaged, research-oriented computer programs have practically eliminated the need for researchers to write complex programs in actual computer languages, such as Fortran or Cobal, in all but the most rare cases. Concerning these modern packages, the most popular and versatile set of programs for survey or testing research is the Statistical Package for the Social Sciences (Nie, et al, 1981). The explanation of the statistical programs, written in lay terms, is clear and very easy to understand.

The Statistical Package for the Social Sciences (SPSS)

This one package serves many statistical analysis needs. (Incidentally, the SPSS manual doubles as a first-rate primer text on statistical analysis as well.) Nearly all universities will have SPSS on their computing system. Consult with computer center personnel regarding the availability and usage of SPSS and acquire the manual.

Table 8.8 depicts a sample SPSS control file (i.e., program) for analyzing a doctoral dissertation. The SPSS manual explains each processing step in great detail, however, a brief explanation for the major commands will be given here. Reference each point discussed below with the matching statement shown in Table 8.8:

13 Typical SPSS Commands:

1   VARIABLE LIST - number of variables (items in the study.

2   INPUT MEDIUM - storage type used for data file (tape, disk, or cards).

3   N OF CASES - number of respondents, if known.

4   INPUT FORMAT - how variables are arranged (order and column width) within the data file.

5   MISSING VALUES - values for respective variables indicating "no response" answers.

6   VAR LABELS - titles for each variable which will appear on printouts.

7   VALUE LABELS - titles for categories of each variable which will appear on print-outs.

8   FREQUENCIES - a "procedure" command calling for frequency distribution; also utilizing "statistics" commands for descriptive statistics on each variable cited in "frequency" command.

9   READ INPUT DATA - mandatory command after first procedure command.

10   CROSSTABS - procedural command to test first null hypothesis (via chi-square).

11   t-TEST - procedural command to test second null hypothesis (via t-test).

12   ONEWAY - procedural command to test unhypothesized findings (via analysis of variance).

13   FINISH - always concludes program.

TABLE 8.8

SPSS SAMPLE PROGRAM

```
FILE NAME        PH.D. (CHILD GUIDANCE CLINIC DATA; 1982)
VARIABLE LIST    V1 TO V24
INPUT MEDIUM     DISK
N OF CASES       157
INPUT FORMAT     FIXED(F2.0,4F1.0,F2.0,F1.0,F2.0,3F1.0,
                 7F2.0,2F1.0,F2.0,2F1.0,F3.0)
MISSING VALUES   V1 TO V12,V15 TO V16,V18 TO V24(0)/V13,V17(99)
VAR LABELS       V1 AGE OF PATIENT AT ENTRY/
                 V2 SEX OF PATIENT/
                 V3 NO. OF SIBLINGS IN FAMILY/
                 V4 ETHNICITY OF PATIENT/
                 V5 EDUCATION OF PATIENT AT ENTRY/
                 V6 PATIENT'S SOURCE OF REFERRAL TO CLINIC/
                 V7 PATIENT'S INSURANCE COVERAGE/
                 V8 PREVIOUS SERVICES HAD BY PATIENT/
                 V9 SCHOOL IMPAIRMENT OF PATIENT/
                 V10 FAMILY IMPAIRMENT OF PATIENT/
                 V11 COMMUNITY IMPAIRMENT OF PATIENT/
                 V12 TOTAL IMPAIRMENT OF PATIENT/
                 V13 FATHER'S GROSS INCOME/
                 V14 MOTHER'S GROSS INCOME/
                 V15 FATHER'S AGE/
                 V16 MOTHER'S AGE/
                 V17 FATHER'S EDUCATION/
                 V18 MOTHER'S EDUCATION/
                 V19 MOTHER'S PROBLEMS WITH PREGNANCY/
                 V20 MOTHER'S DEPRESSION AFTER PREGNANCY/
                 V21 MONTHS OF PREGNANCY/
                 V22 SIBLING POSITION OF PATIENT/
                 V23 MARITAL STATUS OF PATIENT'S PARENTS/
                 V24 PATIENT I.D. NUMBER/
VALUE LABELS     V2 (1)MALE (2)FEMALE
                 V3 (1)ONE (2)TWO (3)THREE (4)FOUR OR MORE
                 V4 (1)WHITE (2)BLACK
                 V5 (1)GRADE SCHOOL (2)SOME HIGH SCHOOL (3)OTHER
                 V6 (6)LOCAL HEALTH DEPT. (8)FAMILY,FRIENDS
                    (9)SELF (10)SCHOOL (12)SOCIAL SERVICES
                    (13)STATE HOSPITAL (15)PUBLIC O.P. SERVICE
                    (16)PRIVATE THERAPIST (17)MISC. INPATIENT SERV.
                    (18)CURCUIT COURT (21)JUV. COURT (23)OTHER
                 V7 (1)INSURED (2)NOT INSURED
                 V8 (1)PUBLIC PSY. HOSPITAL (2)OTHER PSY. HOSPITAL
                    (3)OTHER M.H. CENTERS (5)OUTPAT M.H. CLINIC
                    (6)PRIVATE M.H. PROG. (7)OTHER, NOT ABOVE
                    (8)THIS CLINIC ONLY (9)COM OF ABOVE W PPH
                    (10)CON OF ABOVE WO PPH (11)NO PREVIOUS SERVICE
                 V9 TO V11 (1)NO IMPAIRMENT (2)MINIMAL (3)MILD
                        (4)MODERATE (5)SEVERE
                 V12 (3)NO IMPAIRMENT (15)SEVERE IMPAIRMENT
                 V13 (1)4 TO 9 THOU (2)10 TO 12 THOU
                     (3)13 TO 15 THOU (4)16 OR MORE THOU
                     (99)REFUSED TO ANSWER
                 V14 (1)2 TO 5 THOU (2)6 TO 8 THOU
                     (3)9 TO 12 THOU (99)REFUSED (0)NO INCOME
                 V15 (1)25-29 YEARS (2)30-39 YEARS
                     (3)40-49 YEARS (4)50 YEARS OR MORE
                 V16 (1)24-30 YEARS (2)24-30 YEARS
                     (3)31-40 YEARS
                 V17 TO V18 (1)GRADE SCHOOL (2)SOME H.S.

                         (3)H.S. GRAD. (4)BEYOND H.S.
                         (99)REFUSED
                 V19 TO V20 (1)NO (2)YES
                 V23 (1)MARRIED (2)DIVORCED (3)SEPARATED
                     (4)NEVER MARRIED (5)OTHER (6)OTHER
FREQUENCIES      GENERAL=V1 TO V24
OPTIONS          3
STATISTICS       1,2,3,4,5
READ INPUT DATA
CROSSTABS        TABLES=V6 BY V2
STATISTICS       1
T-TEST           GROUPS=V2/VARIABLES=V9 TO V12
ONEWAY           V9 TO V12 BY V6(1,4)/
                 RANGES=DUNCAN(.05)/
OPTIONS          6
STATISTICS       1,2,3
FINISH
```

177

Test Scoring Packages

If a data analysis or pilot study involves test scoring, item analysis, or internal consistency reliability measurements, a test scoring computer package is required. There are literally hundreds available, mainly at local or intermediate school districts throughout the country. Some larger university computer systems also have test scoring packages available. The best package for test scoring, item analysis, or reliability measurement is LERTAP (Nelson, 1974), developed in New Zealand, but available throughout the United States.

LERTAP is best because it allows the researcher total freedom in setting up the input format of the variables. No special answer sheets are needed, and the programming is quite simple. The item analysis and reliability analyses sections are unsurpassed. Total scores for the test(s) given can even be printed out or kept in computer storage for later statistical analysis, perhaps by the SPSS package.

Use LERTAP if it can be found. As a last resort, find and use another test scoring and analysis package. Review the package's capabilities before designing the final instrumentation, as the data input format may be stringently dictated by the package's design limitations.

WHAT HAPPENS INSIDE THE COMPUTER?

At first, a student or other researcher may very understandably ask, "Who cares?" However, a brief discussion in very general and simplistic terms will help the investigator better understand the tools, and hence the potential, of what they are working with, in terms of analytical power. Every researcher needs to know at least a little about this major tool.

As has already been discussed, raw data enters the computer by cards, tape, direct key-entry, or scan sheet onto a disk; this constitutes the data file. Next, a control file (Table 8.8), usually entered from cards or from a terminal, is created and generally also stored on disk. The computer's central processing unit (i.e., "brain") utilizes the data file in conjunction with the control file to produce an output file consisting of SPSS, LERTAP, or whatever style, analysis.

The output file can be stored on disk or tape, and/or printed out on computer paper. Obviously, for analytical and review purposes, a common output file "print-out" on paper is most useful. Today, various types of printers are available, including the superb Xerox printers. These printers offer 8½" x 11" paper sheets, multi-color stock, and even different typeface styles. Contact computer center personnel at your installation for information before running the actual output file print-outs. Always get two copies of valuable output file print-outs and reserve one copy for security. Do not store the output file copies together.

Table 8.9 illustrates, in very simplistic terms, basic computer operations. Review the table and try to understand the flow of events between the various components. Don't be apprehensive; the table is much easier to follow and understand than it looks.

ANALYZING COMPUTER PRINT-OUTS

After receiving a print-out, the researcher is often shocked by the avalanche of snowy white computer paper. However, voluminous print-outs of statistical findings can be made easier to handle by using this Three-Point Print-Out Review Process:

1   The print-out will correspond to the program and therefore should already be in a logical order, as outlined earlier in this chapter. First, go through the frequency distribution tables for each variable and ensure that all data responses are appropriate.

2   Review the various statistical tables for hypothesized and unhypothesized findings.

3   When confronted with the identical statistical procedure performed repeatedly on different variables, construct full-page summary sheets and indicate which tests are statistically significant. Such summary tables can even be used in the final research report in many cases. Table 8.10 illustrates a summary table involving numerous Pearson correlations, while Table 8.11 depicts a summary table of multiple chi-square tests. Notice how only the statistically significant findings are highlighted. All statistical tests performed would be listed as shown in Tables 8.10 and 8.11. In writing

the final report, all the null hypotheses findings would be discussed, while usually only the statistically significant unhypothesized findings would be presented. (More about writing in the next chapter.)

SUMMARY

Chapter 8 has covered the aspects of computerizing data and programming. Recommendations regarding instrument development for computer compatibility and organization of data format were presented. Suggestions regarding the use of SPSS and LERTAP were made, with an example illustrated of the former. A step-by-step general computer programming guide was provided. Next, a brief primer concerning computer operations was presented, and finally, practical suggestions regarding the analysis and handling of print-outs were made. Suggested readings are provided. Checklist VIII follows and should be completed before continuing further.

TABLE 8.9

THE COMPUTER PROCESS ILLUSTRATED

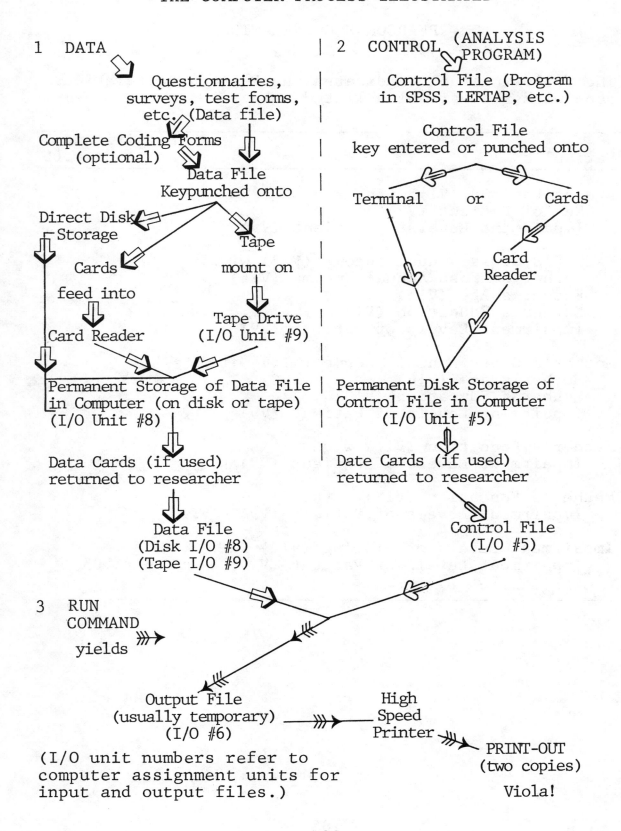

1 DATA
   Questionnaires,
   surveys, test forms,
   etc. (Data file)
Complete Coding Forms
   (optional)
           Data File
           Keypunched onto
Direct Disk
  Storage
    Cards   Tape
    feed into   mount on
Card Reader   Tape Drive
                       (I/O Unit #9)

Permanent Storage of Data File
in Computer (on disk or tape)
(I/O Unit #8)

Data Cards (if used)
returned to researcher

           Data File
           (Disk I/O #8)
           (Tape I/O #9)

2 CONTROL (ANALYSIS PROGRAM)
   Control File (Program
   in SPSS, LERTAP, etc.)
       Control File
   key entered or punched onto

Terminal   or   Cards

                       Card
                       Reader

Permanent Disk Storage of
Control File in Computer
(I/O Unit #5)

Date Cards (if used)
returned to researcher

           Control File
           (I/O #5)

3 RUN
   COMMAND
     yields

           Output File   High
           (usually temporary)   Speed
           (I/O #6)   Printer
                                       PRINT-OUT
                                       (two copies)
(I/O unit numbers refer to
computer assignment units for   Viola!
input and output files.)

181

TABLE 8.10

SUMMARY TABLE OF

PEARSON'S CORRELATIONS

The following table indicates the Pearson correlations
done with the variables listed:

Variables	Significance at alpha =.05

Age of Patient (V1) with:
    Sex of Patient (V2)
    Impairment Levels of Patient (V9)	

Father's Gross Annual Income (V13) with:
    Mother's Gross Annual Income (V14)
    Father's Age (V15)
    Father's Education (V17) ....
    Impairment Levels of Patient (V9)
	p < .05

Mother's Gross Annual Income (V14) with:
    Mother's Age (V16)
    Mother's Education (V18)
    Impairment Levels of Patient (V9)	

Father's Education (V17) with: Impairment Levels of Patient (V9)	
Mother's Education (V18) with: Impairment Levels of Patient (V9)	
Impairment Levels of Sibling (V12) with: Impairment Levels of Patient (V9)	p < .05

TABLE 8.11

SUMMARY TABLE OF TWO-WAY CHI-SQUARE TESTS

The following table indicates the two-way analyses done with the variables listed:

Variables	Significance at alpha =.05
Age of Patient (V1) with:	
Patient's Source of Referral to Clinic (V6)	
Patient's Insurance Coverage (V7)	
Previous Services Received by Patient (V8)	
School Impairment (V9)	p < .05
Family Impairment (V10)	
Community Impairment (V11)	
Total Impairment (V12)	p < .05
Sex of Patient (V2) with:	
Patient's Source of Referral to Clinic (V6)	
Patient's Insurance Coverage (V7)	
Previous Services Received by Patient (V8)	
School Impairment (V9)	
Family Impairment (V10)	
Community Impairment (V11)	
Total Impairment (V12)	p < .05
Mother's Physical Problems with Pregnancy (V19)	
Months of Pregnancy (V21)	

REFERENCES AND SUGGESTED READINGS

The list below has been selected with the utmost care. The listing has been purposely limited to only those texts which are of great practical and useful value to most doctoral or professional researchers. Not every entry may be still in print, but generally a search to locate such a book will be very worthwhile. Entries denoted with a double asterisk (**) are those highly recommended for the topic specified. Parenthetical comments for each entry are added by this author.

Adams, J. M. and Haden, D. H. Computers: Appreciation, Applications, Implications - An Introduction. New York: John Wiley and Sons, 1973.

(A good introduction to how computers work; no programming experience required.)

Klecka, Nie, N., Hull, C. SPSS Primer. New York: McGraw-Hill, 1982.

(Summary of SPSS operations.)

**Nelson, L. Guide to LERTAP Use and Interpretation. Dunedin, New Zealand: Education Department, University of Otago, 1974.

(If LERTAP is unavailable at your computer installation, find something similar. This book is still worth finding first for comparative purposes, if you need to select a similar test scoring program later.)

**Nie, N., Hull, C., Jenkins, J., Steinbrenner, K., and Bent, D. Statistical Package for the Social Sciences, Combined Edition. New York: McGraw-Hill, 1981.

("Must" reading for those using SPSS in their statistical analysis. No exceptions! The combined edition includes the manual, update, and pocket guide.)

Nie, N. and Hull, C. SPSS Pocket Guide, Release 9. New York: McGraw-Hill, 1981.

(A small, quick-reference guide.)

**Nie, N. and Hull, C. <u>SPSS Update 7-9</u>. New York:
    McGraw-Hill, 1982.

    (An important update of the basic 1975 volume;
    "must" reading.)

Norusis, M. J. <u>SPSS Introductory Guide: Basic Statis-
    tics and Operations</u>. New York: McGraw-Hill,
    1982.

    (As the title implies, a basic introduction to
    SPSS.)

CHECKLIST VIII

( )   1.   Develop your instruments to be computer compatible, using Tables 8.1 and 8.6 as guides.

( )   2.   Decide on which medium (cards, tape, direct key-entry scan sheets) to be used for data input. What is the rationale for this choice?

( )   3.   Develop the input format for the data using the Data Dictionary Eight-Step List (Table and Worksheet 8.7).

( )   4.   Use SPSS for most data analysis. Review the Four-Point Recommended Programming Sequence.

( )   5.   Study the 13 Typical SPSS Commands and Table 8.8 carefully.

( )   6.   Locate and use LERTAP for most test scoring, item analysis, or reliability evaluation. If LERTAP is unavailable, use a similar procedure but beware of input format limitations.

( )   7.   Understand the basic workings of a computer system as depicted in Table 8.9.

( )   8.   Use the Three-Point Print-Out Review Process to analyze, in logical order, the printed output file. (See Tables 8.10 and 8.11 for charting examples.)

( )   9.   Review the Suggested Readings and comments.

Writing the Final Report

INTRODUCTION

This chapter will review and discuss the production of final research reports. Perhaps the most inconsistent aspect of doctoral or professional research work, this author has been repeatedly amazed over the past few years at the numerous types of writing formats considered "standard" for such academic or professional documents.

Unfortunately, it is impossible to present a writing outline that will please all advisors or audiences. Nonetheless, this chapter will aid tremendously in guiding the researcher to an excellent final document, very close to the form which should be finally approved in the majority of cases.

It is suggested that a dissertation or professional report be completed as fully as possible both before and during the collection and analysis of the data. In many instances, finished reports up to the findings section can be completed even before all data has been collected. As a general rule, the more of the final report completed before the data collection phase, the better. Oftentimes, parts of the original research proposal can be used extensively in the final report, particularly in areas of problem statements and literature reviews.

Give advisors or others plenty of time (i.e., 4-6 weeks) to read your draft(s). Monitor their progress unobtrusively. It is strongly advisable to submit drafts of your final document or proposal in as finished a form as possible to your audience, unless firmly instructed otherwise.

DOCTORAL MORAL XII

The more polished, professional, and complete your document appears, the less it will be altered by others.

THE OPTIMUM DOCTORAL/
PROFESSIONAL RESEARCH REPORT

The optimum research report outline, with accompanying headings, is depicted in Table 9.1. Each element in the outline is discussed additionally in the text. Take time and review Table 9.1 very carefully. Use Worksheet 9.1 to later outline your own final document.

TABLE 9.1

THE OPTIMUM DISSERTATION/PROFESSIONAL

RESEARCH REPORT OUTLINE

i-1   Title Page

i-2   Copyright Statement

i-3   Abstract

i-4   Acknowledgements

i-5   Table of Contents

i-6   List of Tables

i-7   List of Illustrations, Diagrams

CHAPTER I - STATEMENT OF THE PROBLEM

   A.   General Background
   B.   Specific Background
   C.   Specific Problem Statement(s)
   D.   Research or Alternate Hypotheses
       (in order of importance)
   E.   Null Hypotheses
       (in order of research hypotheses)

CHAPTER II - LITERATURE REVIEW

   A.   General Review of Broad Field
   B.   Specific Review Relative to Each Research
       Hypothesis (in order of same)

TABLE 9.1 (continued)

CHAPTER III - METHODS AND PROCEDURES

A. Research Design
   (including Time Line)
B. Instrument Development or Selection
   1. Validity
   2. Reliability
   3. Item Analysis
C. Sampling Technique
D. Data Collection Methodology
E. Data Computerization Process
   (including Coding, Editing, Keypunching,
   etc.)
F. Statistical Analysis Model to be Used
   1. For Hypotheses (in order of same)
   2. For Unhypothesized Findings

CHAPTER IV - FINDINGS

A. Hypothesized Findings
   (state each null hypothesis, then its
   respective finding(s) in their original
   order)
B. Unhypothesized Findings
   (in order of interest or importance)
C. Non-Statistical Findings
D. Subject Description
   (usually optional)

CHAPTER V - CONCLUSIONS, LIMITATIONS & RECOMMENDATIONS

A. Review of Chapters I-IV
   (brief—this can double as the "abstract")
B. Conclusions from Hypothesized Findings
   (in exact order of same)
C. Conclusions from Unhypothesized Findings
   (in exact order of same)
D. Compare and Contrast Statistical Conclusions
   to Non-Statistical Conclusions
E. Limitations
F. Recommendations
   1. Programmatic Recommendations (relative
      to the topic, based upon the study's
      findings and conclusions)

TABLE 9.1 (continued)

2.   Future Research Recommendations
     (relative to the improvement of future
     studies, based largely upon the
     limitations)

i-8   APPENDICES (all sections optional)

     A.   Detailed Data Tables
     B.   Raw Data Files
     C.   Detailed Computer Information
     D.   Glossary of Technical Terminology

i-9   REFERENCES

i-10   BIBLIOGRAPHY

     (sometimes may be combined with references)

i-11   AUTOBIOGRAPHICAL STATEMENT

———————

Additional Note:

     Occasionally, a very short introductory
     paragraph and summary ending paragraph
     may be inserted to start and end each
     chapter.

Each content area shown in the outline will now be discussed, using its respective number and letter code as previously shown in Table 9.1.

FRONT MATTER

i-1, Title Page

The title page should be designed in standard form. For dissertations, contact the advisor or graduate office for a copy of this format. The title should describe the topic of the research without being pretentious. Note the example below:

AN ANALYSIS OF THE EFFECTS OF FORMAL, TENURED-TEACHER
EVALUATION ON TEACHERS' PERCEPTIONS
OF QUALITY OF WORK LIFE

by

(Name)

A DISSERTATION

Submitted to the Graduate School
of   (Name)   University,
(City, State)
in partial fulfillment of the requirements
for the degree of

DOCTOR OF PHILOSOPHY
1982

MAJOR: GENERAL ADMINISTRATION AND SUPERVISION

APPROVED BY:

. . . .
Adviser   Date

. . . .

. . . .

. . . .

i-2, Copyright Statement

Every dissertation and nearly all professional research must carry a copyright statement. Word this statement exactly as shown below:

i-3, Abstract

Using a format guide from the advisor, graduate office, or previous professional report, prepare an abstract or summary of the study. The abstract should summarize Chapters I through V of the final document.

<u>Length Range</u>:   2-5 pages, all report typing double spaced, 1-1½" margins. Regarding dissertations, see your graduate office for specific page layout.

<u>Verb Tense</u>:   Past

i-4, Acknowledgements

Be sure to thank the following people, in this order:

(√)

_____ Advisor
_____ Committee Members
_____ Scholarship/Fellowship   } in dissertations only
      Committees, as necessary

_____ Field Assistants, other data collection personnel
_____ Technical Support Staff
_____ Typist(s)
_____ Clerk(s)
_____ Family, Friends (i.e., those who put up with you during the project!)

<u>Length Range</u>: 1-2 pages   <u>Verb Tense</u>: Past

192

i-5, Table of Contents

List chapter titles and major headings only. Generally do not list subheadings.

i-6, i-7, Listings of Tables Illustrations, Diagrams

List titles including both the table numbers and page numbers on which the tables appear. Table titles should be in past tense.

MAJOR HEADINGS

Chapter I - Statement of the Problem

A-E   Discuss each major heading as shown in Table 9.1. Focus down to the research hypotheses, starting first from the general problem under study and then to the specific issues the study will address. Throughout Chapter I, the writer should be building a case for why the research hypotheses are worth studying and why the research hypotheses are stated as they are. Use references and quotes generously to make your points. State all research hypotheses, together with respective null hypotheses in order of importance. Much of Chapter I may have already appeared as part of the original research proposal in the case of a dissertation. In short, Chapter I sells the need and value of the study, together with research hypotheses.

Length Range: 12-30 pages
Verb Tense: Past (preferred) or Present

Chapter II - Literature Review

A-B   First, discuss only the major contributors to the general field of study (doctoral students, this is usually your "major" area). Secondly, review literature specific to the study. A common question always arises: How many references are "enough?" Obviously, this is largely dependent upon the topic under study, but a total of 10 to 30 references is common. If necessary to delimit the reference list, use only major contributing authors and/or most recent article dates, as a general rule.

Additionally, make sure that the literature review relates clearly to the research hypotheses. Present the literature review relative to the order of the research hypotheses. Stay focused, stay in strict order, and please don't ramble!

Length Range: 10-40 pages
Verb Tense: Past

Chapter III - Methods and Procedures

A-F   This chapter describes the basic foundation of the study in terms of design, instrumentation, sampling, data collection, and statistical analysis. First, describe the research design, including diagrams if appropriate. Also, include the time line for the research in this section.

A full discussion of instrumentation should follow. Include selection criteria for the instrument, together with validity, reliability, and, optionally, item analysis information. Next, sampling technique, data collection methodology, computerization processes, and statistical analysis procedures should be discussed, in that order. For statistical tests, illustrate a model of the equation and describe why each statistical test was selected.

Length Range: 25-60 pages
Verb Tense: Past or Present

Chapter IV - Findings

This chapter represents the heart of the study in statistical terms, but is often really quite misunderstood. Moreover, note that the entire chapter concerns only findings. It is an extreme temptation, but do not yet conclude from the findings in this chapter. This chapter merely describes what was found, without interpretation.

Such a strict narrative of findings usually creates a reasonably dry text, but it does represent proper scientific style. Regarding findings, present only statistical tables of precise relevance; detailed auxiliary tables are to be placed into Appendix A. In the text, do not simply restate what the table already depicts; elaborate on the findings' tables, yet don't interpret what the findings may mean. After completing the chapter on findings, re-read it to ensure that conclusions are not accidently mentioned or even insinuated.

Follow a four-point procedure in writing Chapter IV. Note that the letters in the left margin follow the outline in Table 9.1.

A   Start with hypothesized findings. Always present the hypothesized findings in order of their original listing in Chapter I. Follow this sequence:

1.   Re-state the null hypothesis ($H_{(0)}$).

2.   Present its respective statistical test(s), alpha level(s), and finding(s).

3.   State whether or not the null hypothesis was rejected.

Continue with the second null hypothesis and maintain the identical three-point reporting pattern. Remember, it is always the null hypotheses which are statistically tested. Each individual null hypothesis has its own statistical test and resultant statistical finding. Handle each null hypothesis separately and in its original order described in the proposal or Chapter I.

B   After completing the hypothesized findings section, present all other unhypothesized statistical findings. Place these in order of importance relative to the research hypotheses. Present only unhypothesized findings which somehow logically relate to the research hypotheses.

C   Include all non-statistical findings. Such sections generally are comprised of respondents' long-answer quotes or face-to-face interview attitudinal responses. Use this section to help complement the statistical findings discussed earlier. Often, interesting similarities or contrasts will emerge when comparing statistical and non-statistical findings. Use the non-statistical findings to add an innovative human dimension to the study's more statistical aspects.

D   As an optional section, a full description of
        sampled respondents (subjects) may be presented
next.   Here the frequency distributions and descriptive
statistics (refer to Chapter VII) for each demographic
variable may be detailed.   This is extremely useful to
readers interested in the specific composition of the
respondent group.   Such information greatly aids other
researchers in establishing accurate replications of the
study.   Depending upon the number of demographic variables collected (e.g., age, sex, race, education, marital status, etc.), this section can become voluminous.
As stated previously, inclusion of this section is generally optional, but it is strongly recommended for a
truly professional research document.   Occasionally,
this demographic description can be placed in Chapter III
or in an appendix.

        <u>Length Range</u>:   5-25 pages
        <u>Verb Tense</u>:   Past

        <u>Chapter V - Conclusions,
        Limitations and Recommendations</u>

A   Start Chapter V by summarizing Chapters I through
        IV.   Since some readers may turn directly to
Chapter V, this introductory summary will provide their
only concise synopsis.   The summary should be no more
than about three pages in length.   This summary should be
used again as part of the report's abstract.

B   Following the introductory summary, interpretations
        and conclusions drawn from the hypothesized find-
ings should be presented, in the exact order of the hypotheses.

C   Next, other conclusions from unhypothesized find-
        ings should be discussed.

D   Lastly, any comparisons or contrasts between
        statistical and non-statistical findings should be
presented.

        Each of the last three aspects cited above (B, C,
and D) should be discussed completely, with sound

rationale for the conclusions derived. Remember, non-significant statistical findings may also yield powerful conclusions. Don't allow only statistically significant test results to control the entire direction of the writing.

While concluding from findings, ask yourself why the results were what they were. Ensure that each and every conclusion drawn is defendable on logical grounds. Caution: Do not over-generalize conclusions to dis-similar subject groups or populations. There is no better way to create a poor Chapter V.

```
DOCTORAL MORAL XIII

If in doubt, always be conservative regarding
the extent to which you conclude from the
                    findings.
```

E   All studies (yes, even yours!) have limitations.
Either in design, sampling, instrumentation, statistics, or something else, every study ever done has had its flaws. When describing the study's limiting factors, be open and honest, but don't destroy yourself! (If the study has been well executed step-by-step, there is nothing to really worry about here.)

F   Concerning recommendations, first divide them into
      two distinct segments. Initially, discuss program-matic recommendations; that is, suggestions that can be directed toward the topic or subjects under study. How should the program be changed? How can the situation be improved? All suggestions, of course, need be directly related back to the study's hypothesized and unhypothe-sized findings and their respective conclusions.

Secondly, present recommendations for further study. What should be done next in researching this area? How can this study's limitations be avoided in future research? What about other designs, instruments, and respondents in future research efforts, etc.? In short, where do we go from here with the research in this field?

Length Range: 10-20 pages
Verb Tense: Past (preferred) or Present

i-8, Appendices

Appendices vary in size, largely dependent upon advisor or audience preferences. Generally, a basic appendices section will contain at least the detailed statistical tables not presented in Chapter IV - Findings.

Additionally, appendices may contain the raw data file listing, detailed computer programs, and a glossary of technical terminology. Use the appendices for any and all of these aspects as needed, however, don't attempt to pad the report with irrelevant information; it's usually far too obvious and very unprofessional. As a rule, if in serious debate about including a certain appendix, leave it out if it's over 20 pages in length, otherwise place it in.

Length Range: 0-100 pages +
Verb Tense: Past (preferred) or Present

i-9, References

References used in the body of the report must, of course, be listed in the traditional style, without exception.

The American Psychological Association (APA) Manual gives numerous examples of correct reference style. Additionally, review completed dissertations for more examples. How to actually denote a reference in the text of the report is discussed in the Writing Style section ahead.

Number of Entries, Common Range: 20-60

i-10, Bibliography

Not to be confused with references, a bibliography presents related material reviewed and studied by the author, but not formally referenced in the text. Some dissertations or professional reports have this list merged with the reference list, which is a usually acceptable practice, however, prior approval of this method is mandatory.

Number of Entries, Common Range: 10-30

i-11, Autobiographical Statement

All dissertations and some professional research reports require a one to three-page biographical review of the author. Present a factual description of your birthplace, education, career direction and overall interests.

<u>Length Range</u>: 1-3 pages
<u>Verb Tense</u>:   Past and Present

YOUR RESEARCH REPORT OUTLINE

Use Worksheet 9.1 to roughly outline your dissertation or research report. In the spaces provided, list specific topics to be addressed and estimate page length for each section. While writing the final report, compare actual topics of discussion and length estimates to those projected earlier. A literary project of this size results in a mammoth writing task. Readjust writing style and length as you proceed. In using Worksheet 9.1, an idea of your progress and writing volume can be continuously monitored. Without this guide, it is easy to lose writing structure, focus, and clarity in the final document.

WRITING STYLE—APA OR TURABIAN?

The American Psychological Association (APA)(1975) and Turabian (1963) publish manuals on formal writing format. These two manuals are the traditional standards established for the writing format of dissertations, professional research reports, and journal articles. In most cases, the graduate school, department, advisor, or audience will dictate which one of the two writing formats is desired. It is well worth purchasing the needed manual well before starting to write. Study the manual closely for format rules, with particular attention given to table, diagram, and quotation format rules. Regarding dissertations, now is also a great time to review the writing format and style of a recently approved report from your advisor or committee. As mentioned earlier, the standard writing formats are altered by many people, so a review of a report recently approved is most valuable. If given a choice of writing style, use APA. The major reason APA is recommended is that it uses a far simpler footnote system. This results in a final document produced at reduced typing expense.

WORKSHEET 9.1

RESEARCH REPORT OUTLINE

Title/Headings	List Topics to be Covered/Comments	Est. Pages
i-1 TITLE PAGE		
i-2 COPYRIGHT STATEMENT		
i-3 ABSTRACT		
i-4 ACKNOWLEDGEMENTS		

200

WORKSHEET 9.1 (continued)

Title/Headings	List Topics to be Covered/Comments	Est. Pages
i-5 TABLE OF CONTENTS		
i-6 LIST OF TABLES		
i-7 LIST OF ILLUSTRATIONS, DIAGRAMS		

201

WORKSHEET 9.1 (continued)

Chapter	Title/Headings	List Topics to be Covered/Comments	Est. Pages
I	STATEMENT OF THE PROBLEM		
	A. General Background		
	B. Specific Background		

202

WORKSHEET 9.1 (continued)

Chapter	Title/Headings	List Topics to be Covered/Comments	Est. Pages
I	STATEMENT OF THE PROBLEM (continued)		
	C. Specific Problem Statements		
	D. Research or Alternate Hypotheses (numbered)		
	E. Null Hypotheses (numbered)		

WORKSHEET 9.1 (continued)

Chapter	Title/Headings	List Topics to be Covered/Comments	Est. Pages
II	LITERATURE REVIEW		
	A. General Review - Broad Field		

WORKSHEET 9.1 (continued)

Chapter	Title/Headings	List Topics to be Covered/Comments	Est. Pages
II	LITERATURE REVIEW (continued)		
	B. Specific Review		

WORKSHEET 9.1 (continued)

Chapter	Title/Headings	List Topics to be Covered/Comments	Est. Pages
III	METHODS AND PROCEDURES		
	A. Research Design		
	B. Instrument Development		
	C. Sampling Technique		

WORKSHEET 9.1 (continued)

Chapter	Title/Headings	List Topics to be Covered/Comments	Est. Pages
III	METHODS AND PROCEDURES (continued)		
	D. Data Collection Methodology		
	E. Data Computerization Processes		
	F. Statistical Analysis		

207

WORKSHEET 9.1 (continued)

Chapter	Title/Headings	List Topics to be Covered/Comments	Est. Pages
IV	FINDINGS		
	A. Hypothesized Findings		
	B. Unhypothesized Findings		

208

WORKSHEET 9.1 (continued)

Chapter	Title/Headings	List Topics to be Covered/Comments	Est. Pages
IV	FINDINGS (continued)		
	C. Non-Statistical Findings		
	D. Subject Description		

WORKSHEET 9.1 (continued)

Chapter	Title/Headings	List Topics to be Covered/Comments	Est. Pages
V	CONCLUSIONS, LIMITATIONS, RECOMMENDATIONS		
	A. Review Chapters I-IV		
	B. Conclusions from Hypothesized Findings		

WORKSHEET 9.1 (continued)

Chapter	Title/Headings	List Topics to be Covered/Comments	Est. Pages
V	CONCLUSIONS, LIMITATIONS, RECOMMENDATIONS (continued)		
	C. Conclusions from Unhypothesized Findings		
	D. Compare and Contrast Statistical Conclusions to Non-Statistical Conclusions		

WORKSHEET 9.1 (continued)

Chapter	Title/Headings	List Topics to be Covered/Comments	Est. Pages
V	CONCLUSIONS, LIMITATIONS, RECOMMENDATIONS (continued)		
	E. Limitations		
	F. Recommendations		

WORKSHEET 9.1 (continued)

Est. Pages	Title/Headings	List Topics to be Covered/Comments
	APPENDICES	
i-8	Detailed Data Tables	
	Raw Data Files	
	Detailed Computer Information	
	Glossary of Technical Terminology	

WORKSHEET 9.1 (continued)

Title/Headings	List Topics to be Covered/Comments	Est. Pages
i-9 REFERENCES	# Entries: _____	
i-10 BIBLIOGRAPHY	# Entries: _____	
i-11 AUTOBIOGRAPHICAL STATEMENT		

GRAPHIC TECHNIQUE RECOMMENDATIONS

In Chapter IV of the final report, researchers with huge amounts of computer output are often perplexed as to how best to present their findings in a compact, yet informative, style. There are a number of ingenious ways to handle this dilemma, depending upon the type of findings to be presented. The presentation of summary tables within the body of the report can greatly simplify the presentation of findings. The inclusion of summary tables in the body of the report does not mean, however, that the detailed statistical analysis should be discarded. Such detail should be either included in the appendix or personally retained by the researcher.

Graphic Techniques for Frequency Distributions

Starting with frequency or frequency percentage distributions, the actual findings can be neatly superimposed on the original instrument form. Table 9.2 illustrates the technique, using frequency percentages.

Graphic Techniques for Descriptive Statistics

Concerning descriptive statistics, the method again involves superimposing selected descriptive statistics on the original instrument(s). Table 9.3 illustrates this procedure. The example uses data regarding the mean scores from many different groups. As shown, the mean scores can be connected by straight lines. Differing lines can differentiate different groups, times, pre/post scores, statistics, etc. Use this presentation style for any descriptive statistic(s) including mean, median, mode, standard deviation, standard error, etc.

TABLE 9.2

GRAPHIC TECHNIQUE FOR FREQUENCY DISTRIBUTIONS

In what ways (if any) have the employees at your site benefited? Check one or more appropriate responses.

__13%__	1.	They haven't benefited.
__44%__	2.	Increased their awareness of youth.
__9%__	3.	Motivated the regular employees to further training.
__19%__	4.	Reduced their workload.
__22%__	5.	Increased interest in their own work.
__6%__	6.	I don't know.
__13%__	7.	Other (please write in) _____

Do you plan to continue participating with the program next year?

__88%__	1.	Yes COMMENTS: _____
__3%__	2.	No _____
__9%__		(No answer)

Why? (Check one or more reasons below.)

__84%__	1.	Program is worthwhile.
__44%__	2.	I like the people involved.
__59%__	3.	My participation is a community service.
__22%__	4.	It is challenging to me.
__-__	5.	I have had problems with the staff.
__3%__	6.	I have had problems with the students.
__3%__	7.	The program is not effective.
__3%__	8.	I don't have time.
__3%__	9.	Other (please write in) _____

TABLE 9.3

GRAPHIC TECHNIQUE FOR DESCRIPTIVE STATISTICS REPORTING

Directions: Most of the questions are to be answered on a scale of numbers from 1 to 5. Read the phrase above and below the numbers so you know what the scale means, then read each question and circle the number which is closest to your opinion. There are no right or wrong answers; your thoughts and feelings are the important things in this survey.

—— Mean
----- Median

1. How well do you feel the (CE)2 Program compares overall with the past school experiences of your daughter or son?

Much Worse   Much Better
1   2   3 (3.48)   4 (4.37)   5

2. If you had it to do over again, would you want your son or daughter to participate in the (CE)2 Program?

Definitely No   Definitely Yes
1   2   3   (4.11)   4 (4.35)   5

3. How well do you think your son or daughter likes the (CE)2 Program compared with past school experiences?

Much Worse   Much Better
1   2   3 (3.40)   4 (4.63)   5

217

Graphic Techniques for
Inferential Statistics

Regarding inferential statistical test results, much can be reported in a summary table. Table 9.4 depicts four examples of t-test reporting. Using a little creativity, the graphic methods shown in Table 9.4 can be used with any statistical test.

Table 9.5 demonstrates an example presenting ANOVA statistical results. If a reduced computer print-out (SPSS, as shown) is not allowed within the report, simply type the boxed sections of the table as shown for a more traditional presentation.

TABLE 9.4

GRAPHIC TECHNIQUES FOR t-TEST REPORTING

EXAMPLE 1 OF 4

V No.	Question: t-Test of Previous Bus Ridership (V2) with:	Group Means		Signifi-cance Value
		Riders (n=100)	Non-Riders (n=95)	
V7	Appearance of Buses rating	1.71	1.88	.27
V8	Bus Reliability rating	1.83	4.13	.00*
V9	Bus Availability rating	2.07	2.31	.28
V10	Bus Stop Location rating	3.06	2.88	.07
V11	Driver Courtesy rating	4.11	1.13	.00*
V12	Bus Shelter rating	3.12	3.07	.53
V96	Age of Respondent	2.01	2.11	.12
V87	Miles to Work, if Employed	1.77	3.80	.01*

* Significant at alpha level .01.

TABLE 9.4 (continued)

EXAMPLE 2 OF 4

	Mean	S.D.	N	t	df	p
Null Hypothesis I - Career Planning						
Experimental	0.14	0.89	22	-1.90	28.08	.07
Control	1.00	1.90	21			
Null Hypothesis II - Economic Factors						
Experimental	1.27	1.75	22	1.64	41	.11
Control	0.24	2.36	21			
Null Hypothesis III - Career Interests						
Experimental	1.27	1.88	22	1.50	41	.14
Control	0.48	1.57	21			
Null Hypothesis IV & V - Job Acquisition						
Experimental	0.09	0.61	22	0.44	27.86	.67
Control	-0.05	1.32	21			
Null Hypothesis VII - Education/Career						
Experimental	0.91	1.41	22	1.22	41	.23
Control	0.33	1.68	21			

TABLE 9.4 (continued)

EXAMPLE 3 OF 4

Test	Mean Pre-Test	Mean Post-Test	Mean Gain
ABLE Vocabulary	6.5281	7.1844	+ .6563*
ABLE Reading	6.9281	7.5438	+ .6156*
ABLE Spelling	5.3791	5.9906	+ .6188*
ABLE Math Computation	4.9125	6.7000	+1.7875*
ABLE Math Problems	5.3219	6.2344	+ .9125*
ABLE Math Total	5.0719	6.4750	+1.4031*
CAT Reading Vocabulary	6.0656	6.4313	+ .3656
CAT Reading Comprehension	4.7000	6.5938	+2.0406*
CAT Reading Total	5.3875	6.5438	+1.1563*
CAT Math Computation	5.3906	6.9625	+1.5719*
CAT Math Concepts	4.9313	6.4656	+1.5344*
CAT Math Total	5.3063	6.7875	+1.4813*

* Significant at alpha level .05.

221

TABLE 9.4 (continued)

GRAPHIC TECHNIQUES FOR t-TEST REPORTING
EXAMPLE 4 OF 4

GROUP 1 - V91   EQ   1.
GROUP 2 - V91   EQ   2.

- - - - - - - - - - - T - T E S T - - - - - - - - - - -

VARIABLE	NUMBER OF CASES	MEAN	STANDARD DEVIATION	STANDARD ERROR	F VALUE	2-TAIL PROB.	POOLED VARIANCE ESTIMATE T VALUE	DEGREES OF FREEDOM	2-TAIL PROB.
V7 APPEARANCE OF BUSES RATING									
GROUP 1	58	7.6207	1.254	0.165					
					1.00	0.988	-0.04	126	0.972
GROUP 2	70	7.6286	1.253	0.150					
V8 BUS RELIABILITY RATING									
GROUP 1	42	7.4762	1.518	0.234					
					1.47	0.183	-1.33	94	0.187
GROUP 2	54	7.8519	1.250	0.170					
V9 BUS AVAILABILITY RATING									
GROUP 1	50	6.3600	2.354	0.333					
					1.09	0.757	-0.76	110	0.447
GROUP 2	62	6.7097	2.459	0.312					
V10 BUS STOP LOCATION RATING									
GROUP 1	46	7.2609	2.134	0.315					
					1.21	0.517	-0.01	104	0.990
GROUP 2	60	7.2667	2.342	0.302					

TABLE 9.5—GRAPHIC TECHNIQUE FOR ANOVA REPORTING

- - - - - - - - - - - - - - O N E W A Y - - - - - - - - - - - - -

VARIABLE V130   HOW MANY YEARS HAVE YOU LIVED IN?

ANALYSIS OF VARIANCE

SOURCE	D.F.	SUM OF SQUARES	MEAN SQUARES	F RATIO	F PROB.
BETWEEN GROUPS	1	15895.1263	15895.1250	221.682	0.0000
WITHIN GROUPS	1905	126593.2813	71.7025		
TOTAL	1906	152488.3750			

GROUP	COUNT	MEAN	STANDARD DEVIATION	STANDARD ERROR
GRP01	1306	9.8683	9.5914	0.2654
GRP02	601	3.6539	5.2503	0.2142
TOTAL	1907	7.9098	8.9445	0.2048
FIXED EFFECTS MODEL			8.4677	0.1939
RANDOM EFFECTS MODEL			4.6849	3.3127

TESTS FOR HOMOGENEITY OF VARIANCES

COCHRANS C = MAX. VARIANCE/SUM(VARIANCES) = 0.7694, P = 0.000 (APPROX.)
BARTLETT-BOX F = 248.210, P = 0.000
MAXIMUM VARIANCE / MINIMUM VARIANCE = 3.337

223

Graphic techniques for chi-square test results can be presented in numerous ways, an example of which is shown in Table 9.6. Again, note that if different statistical tests are used than those shown in the examples, simply use the graphic ideas to create similar summary tables.

Finally, report non-statistical findings from personal or group interviews using any of the suggested formats shown in Table 9.7. These formats are self-explanatory.

Note that all the tables illustrated in this section are recommended formats based upon years of dissertation and research experience, but they by no means represent the only methods by which findings could be summarized in a tabular form.

EIGHT CRITICAL GUIDELINES IN
DISSERTATION OR PROFESSIONAL
RESEARCH WRITING

Follow these Eight Critical Guidelines in Writing a Dissertation or Report:

1   Follow graduate office (or other) rules for paper weight, margins, and other related production aspects.

2   In writing a document of this size and complexity, maintain a strong outline, using Table 9.1 and Worksheet 9.1, and follow it exactly. Check to ensure that the logical flow of the outline is equally evident in the written document.

3   In discussing tables, diagrams, or illustrations in Chapter IV, do not simply restate what the table already indicates. Elaborate on the findings, but be careful not to conclude until Chapter V.

4   The word "data" is usually considered plural—not singular:

WRONG: The data was from a 5th grade math class.
RIGHT: The data were from a 5th grade math class.

5   Consistently maintain the recommended verb tenses. Do not mix verb tenses in any one section or chapter. Double-check all tenses; it's very easy to overlook errors in this aspect.

6   Do not pad the narrative or tabular sections of the report. Keep the writing style clear and concise. It is generally quite obvious to an experienced reader and it always appears unprofessional.

7   Indent and single space long quotes; see the appropriate manual (APA or Turabian).

8   List only references and bibliography entries that have actually been utilized. Keep the number of entries reasonable. Quality of the entries is generally far more impressive than the quantity.

DOCTORAL MORAL XIV

You only need one final document. Stay intense on your massive writing project, but don't rush it.

SUMMARY

Chapter 9 has detailed writing format and processes. The optimum outline form was presented, together with a discussion of graphics presentations, writing style, and critical writing guidelines. Complete Worksheet 9.1 and ensure a strong structure while writing the final document. As usual, complete Checklist IX before continuing to the final chapter.

TABLE 9.6

GRAPHIC TECHNIQUE FOR CHI-SQUARE TEST REPORTING

Question: Previous Bus Ridership (Yes or No) (V2), crosstabulated with:

V No.	Question	Significance Value
V74	Will you ride if gas $1.50?	.04*
V75	Will you ride if gas $2.00?	.05*
V76	Will you ride if rationing?	.09
V77	If fare increase, keep from riding?	.41
V78	Need go downtown after 3 p.m.?	.01*
V79	Interested in bus to downtown after 3 p.m.?	.01*
V80	Need go out of downtown before 3 p.m.?	.24
V81	Interested in bus out of downtown before 3 p.m.?	.10
V82	Radio station (music) type?	.71
V84	Are you household head	.65
V85	Own or rent residence?	.65
V88	Does bus go by work location?	.00*
V89	Within 3 years; think you will ride GRATA?	.00*
V90	Car available when needed?	.00*
V91	Sex of respondent?	.99
V94	City quadrant code?	.05*

226

* Significant at alpha level .05.

TABLE 9.7

TECHNIQUES FOR PERSONAL INTERVIEW REPORTING

(NON-STATISTICAL)

STYLE 1 OF 2

EXCERPTS FROM . . .

Interview 2; Male Respondent, Age 10

Interviewer	You said that your parents trust you and respect your feelings?
Respondent	Yes. They let me give my opinion, although I'm not sure how much difference it really makes.
Interviewer	You mean that they usually make the final decisions?
Respondent	Well, we all talk about things together. I can talk to my parents. Maybe they had the same problems I'm having now and they would know what to do, but yeah, they usually make the final decision.
Interviewer	Is this different behavior on the part of your parents?
Respondent	Not really, although I wish my family could all do more stuff together. Everybody seems to have separate things to do.
Interviewer	Do you ever talk of drugs and drug use with your parents?
Respondent	Yes. My parents think drugs are bad for you. They say we shouldn't use them and we might get hurt on them. Maybe people use drugs because they are nervous or something.

TABLE 9.7 (continued)

STYLE 2 OF 2

Quotes chosen by the psychological consultant broadly reflect the general nature of responses given by the students. Below is listed the first question and its respective responses:

> 1. Did the initial counseling at the employment center prepare you for the job training?

YES

- I was able to learn and accept negative comments without falling apart or blowing up. I can accept criticism much better.

- The talk sessions were especially good. We discussed aspects of job maintenance, and how you should act on a job. We learned how to consider other people's thoughts and feelings. You need to do that if you're gonna want to be treated with respect yourself.

- They built up my self-confidence. Being cool got you nowhere. Becoming aware of myself as a person is where it's at.

- I learned about flexibility, self-motivation, punctuality and self-control. My whole attitude towards myself, others and the job got real good.

NO

- I felt that the counseling was very poor—it was dull, too.

- The counselors were bad—always late!

- They were always against me; other guys got better training.

REFERENCES AND SUGGESTED READINGS

The list below has been selected with the utmost care. The listing has been purposely limited to only those texts which are of a great practical and useful value to most doctoral or professional researchers. Not every entry may be still in print, but generally a search to locate such a book will be very worthwhile. Entries denoted with a double asterisk (**) are those highly recommended for the topic specified. Parenthetical comments for each entry are added by this author.

Martin, Roy. Writing and Defending a Thesis or Dissertation in Psychology and Education. Springfield, Illinois: Charles C. Thomas Publishers, 1980.

(A small paperback with some fine advice.)

**Publication Manual of the American Psychological Association, 2nd ed. Washington: American Psychological Assoc., 1975.

(If using the APA writing style, this book is "must" reading! No exceptions!)

** Turabian, K.L. A Manual for Writers of Term Papers, Theses, and Dissertations, 4th ed. Chicago: University of Chicago Press, 1973.

(If using the Turabian writing style, this book is "must reading"—no exceptions!)

** Turabian, K.L. Student's Guide for Writing College Papers, 2nd ed. Chicago: University of Chicago Press, 1963.

(An excellent book to consult if writing shorter research reports.)

CHECKLIST IX

( ) 1. Carefully re-read the introduction to this chapter. Submit a polished draft to the advisor or others well ahead of deadlines.

( ) 2. Study <u>The Optimum Dissertation/Professional Research Outline</u> (Table 9.1). Review the text explaining each section as needed.

( ) 3. Complete Worksheet 9.1. Don't rush.

( ) 4. Decide on either the APA or Turabian writing style. Advisor or audience approval is mandatory.

( ) 5. Study all graphic techniques presented. Invent your own graphic displays if desired, but do so carefully.

( ) 6. Find out if computer printed tables will be allowable in your final draft.

( ) 7. Complete the <u>Eight Critical Guidelines in Dissertation or Professional Research Writing</u>.

( ) 8. Review the Suggested Readings and comments.

The Final Report Presentation

INTRODUCTION

The final step in all dissertations and in most other professional research reports is to personally present the final document. Particularly for doctoral students, this presentation will always be a trying experience. Even if complete books were written regarding the presentation, the final oral defense and presentation would still be a dreaded ordeal. This chapter unfortunately cannot address all the emotional aspects involved in final presentations, although those elements are recognized as being very real and are certainly not underrated in their importance. This chapter will offer suggestions, based upon numerous doctoral and professional experiences, that should enable the researcher to make an outstanding presentation, despite the emotional pressure.

BEFORE THE FINAL PRESENTATION

Before discussing the presentation itself, what materials should the researcher prepare for the meeting? First, an unbound copy of the dissertation or report must be supplied to each committee member. Use high quality paper stock and superior duplicating equipment (e.g., Xerox 9200 copier or similar) for these documents. (Frankly, this is no time to be economical.)

Before the meeting, establish a system of non-verbal communication between yourself and your advisor. Learn these signals and use them throughout the presentation.

Use plastic tabs on chapter and major heading pages on your copy. If fielding questions, you will then be able to find the needed information quickly and professionally. Keep an extra Table of Contents and Listing of Tables at your side.

Dress conservatively. This is of particular importance for doctoral dissertation presentations. A quick skim of <u>Dress for Success</u> (Molloy, 1975) or <u>The Woman's Dress for Success Book</u> (Molloy, 1977) is a good idea. Both the report and your personal image must dictate professionalism.

```
┌─────────────────────────────────────────────┐
│                                             │
│             DOCTORAL MORAL XV               │
│                                             │
│   The more completely and quicker a student image │
│    is exchanged for a professional image, the │
│                   better.                   │
│                                             │
└─────────────────────────────────────────────┘
```

DURING THE FINAL PRESENTATION

Initially, the researcher should present an overview of the study. Outline on paper or cards the Abstract (or the Introduction to Chapter V). Next, complete Worksheet 10.1 and use it as an outline for your opening overview. Keep this opening overview about 15 minutes in length and speak slowly. Time allotments per topic are shown on the Worksheet; use them! Maintain equal eye contact with all committee members as you speak. Stay in close eye contact with your advisor throughout the meeting.

After the overview, the group will have questions, comments, or criticisms. It is so very important here that composure be maintained. Answer only the question asked; do not ramble responses endlessly. The committee is usually just as interested in how well you handle questions and conflicts as it is interested in the actual research findings. If you are unsure of an answer, admit it calmly. Don't bluff! Always concentrate on your poise and delivery as well as on what you are saying.

Practice your delivery using sample questions from friends or peers. Better still, stage a full rehearsal session with a recent doctoral graduate friend acting as a committee member. This may seem silly, but it works.

SUMMARY

Just as you perhaps sold your original research idea to your advisor or audience, you are now selling the results, and yourself, in the final presentation. Remember that in the majority of cases, the final presentation causes more anxiety than it deserves. Re-read the 15 Doctoral Morals as repeated in Table 10.1. Complete Checklist X and review the chapter as necessary. If you have carefully utilized this guidebook and honestly completed the checklists, the final presentation should really be only a formality.

WORKSHEET 10.1

ORAL PRESENTATION OUTLINE—

15 MINUTES OF OPENING REMARKS

> Maintain equal eye contact and emit confidence! If you don't know the answer to a question, <u>admit it</u>. Don't bluff!

Fill in keywords as your guide. Do <u>not</u> read a prepared statement:

1 Why are you studying this topic?   (2 minutes)

    A. _____   D. _____

    B. _____   E. _____

    C. _____   F. _____

2 How was the study designed?   (1 minute)

    A. _____   D. _____

    B. _____   E. _____

    C. _____   F. _____

3 Who (what) was sampled and how?   (1 minute)

    A. _____   D. _____

    B. _____   E. _____

    C. _____   F. _____

4 What instruments were used?   (1 minute)

    A. _____   D. _____

    B. _____   E. _____

    C. _____   F. _____

5   What did you find, in original
    order of null hypotheses?   (4 minutes)

        A. _____   D. _____
        B. _____   E. _____
        C. _____   F. _____

6   What do you conclude?   (3 minutes)

        A. _____   D. _____
        B. _____   E. _____
        C. _____   F. _____

7   What do you recommend for changes
    and/or improvements to the field
    or for future studies?   (2 minutes)

        A. _____   D. _____
        B. _____   E. _____
        C. _____   F. _____

Other Reminders or Notes:

```
╔═══════════════════════════════════════════════════╗
║                                                   ║
║                  TABLE 10.1                       ║
║                                                   ║
║         THE 15 DOCTORAL MORALS REVISITED          ║
║                                                   ║
╚═══════════════════════════════════════════════════╝
```

Review each of the 15 Doctoral Morals as they were presented in this guidebook. Re-read sections as necessary.

<u>Moral</u>   <u>Page</u>

I.   After a few thousand hours of   9
     investment, a researcher deserves
     to have a satisfying final
     product.

II. If given a choice, always design   39
     measurable and testable hypo-
     theses; it will greatly strengthen
     the research and reduce potential
     problems later. Share the
     research and null hypotheses with
     your advisor as soon as possible!

III. If attempts are made to cover up   47
     the research design flaws, per the
     Nine-Point Design Danger List, you
     are now <u>officially</u> on thin ice!

IV. Criterion-related validity is a   59
     very useful empirical approach,
     but only if the criterion itself
     is valid.

V.   A small volume of good data is   90
     worth much more than a large volume
     of poor data!

VI. Sample a group large enough to give   115
     credibility to the research, but
     small enough to handle.

VII. Of course, certain variables (e.g.,   123
     sex, race, religion) are categorical
     by nature, but whenever given a
     choice, <u>always</u> collect data in its

TABLE 10.1 (continued)

Moral		Page
	continuous form. Continuous data can be transformed later into categorical data, if desired. It just doesn't work the other way around!	
VIII.	Because two variables are significantly related, they do not necessarily _cause_ each other to vary.	141
IX.	As the significance value found goes _down_, the chances of the null hypothesis being true goes _down_ and, hence, the chances of a real difference or relationship existing in the data goes _up_.	146
X.	In a soundly designed study, the true worth of the research has nothing to do with whether or not statistically significant outcomes were found. Finding no statistically significant results can be very "significant," depend-upon the interpretation of the results.	147
XI.	Doing no study is better than doing an unethical one.	148
XII.	The more polished, professional, and complete your document appears, the less it will be altered by others.	187
XIII.	If in doubt, always be conservative regarding the extent to which you conclude from the findings.	197
XIV.	You only need one final document. Stay intense on your massive writing project, but don't rush it.	225
XV.	The more completely and quicker a student image is exchanged for a professional image, the better.	232

REFERENCES AND SUGGESTED READINGS

The list below has been selected with the utmost care. The listing has been purposely limited to only those texts which are of a great practical and useful value to most doctoral or professional researchers. Not every entry may be still in print, but generally a search to locate such a book will be very worthwhile. Entries denoted with a double asterisk (**) are those highly recommended for the topic specified. Parenthetical comments for each entry are added by this author.

Carnegie, D. How to Win Friends and Influence People. New York: Simon and Schuster, 1936.

(A classic, probably because it works. An on-going development of the skills outlined in this book just may help things go more smoothly at the final oral presentation.)

Martin, Roy. Writing and Defending a Thesis or Dissertation in Psychology and Education. Springfield, Illinois: Charles C. Thomas Publishers, 1980.

(A small paperback with some fine advice.)

Molloy, J. T. Dress for Success. New York: P. H. Wyden, 1975.

(For men concerned about proper attire and appearance at the final oral presentation.)

Molloy, J. T. The Woman's Dress for Success Book. Chicago: Follett, 1977.

(For women concerned about proper attire and appearance at the final oral presentation.)

CHECKLIST X

( ) 1. Review the 15 Doctoral Morals (Table 10.1).

( ) 2. Stage a full rehearsal with a recently graduated student, peer, or friend.

( ) 3. Prepare unbound copies of the final report for all expected meeting members and yourself. Do not use the original copy.

( ) 4. Use plastic tabs to highlight chapters and major headings in your copy of the final report.

( ) 5. Keep an extra Table of Contents and Listing of Tables at your side during the meeting.

( ) 6. Dress conservatively.

( ) 7. Prepare an oral introduction using Worksheet 10.1. Try to keep this opening summary in the 10-15 minute range.

( ) 8. Keep in good eye contact with all meeting members. If a doctoral student, maintain frequent eye contact with your advisor to stay close for support.

( ) 9. Field questions confidently and honestly.

( ) 10. After successfully completing the presentation, celebrate!

INDEX

A

Abstract, writing of, 192
Acknowledgements, writing of, 192
Alpha level, 145-147, 195
Americal Psychological Association (APA), 199
Analysis of variance
   general, 137-140
   graphics for, 223
Anonymity of subjects, 45
ANOVA, see Analysis of Variance
Appendices, design of, 198
Attrition, 45
Autobiographical statement, writing of, 199

B

Bibliographies, see References and Bibliographies
Budgeting, economic factors in research, see Cost of
   Studies
Buro's Books in Print, 25

C

Categorical data, see Data Types
Checklists, xviii
Chi-square
   general, 137-139, 144
   graphics for, 224, 226
   summary table, 183
Complex group stratification, 44
Computer
   cards, 155-165
   coding forms, 155-164
   data input, storage, 160, 164-173, 178
   general usage, 155, 178-181
   input format, 165
   process, illustrated, 181
Conclusions, writing of, 196-197
Confidentiality of subjects, 45
Contingency coefficient, 137-139, 145

Continuous data, see Data Types
Control file, computerized, 166, 174
Copyright statement, writing of, 192
Correlation coefficients
    and reliability measurements, 62, 66-67
    biserial correlation, 68-72
    point-biserial correlation, 68-72
    see also Pearson correlation
Costs of studies, 46, 48-49

D

Data collection, general, 105, 110
Data, falsifying, 148
Data file, computerized, 166, 174
Data types
    nominal, 127-127, 136-139, 166, 172
    ordinal, 126-127, 136-139, 166
    interval, 126-127, 136-139, 166, 172
    ratio, 126-127, 136-139, 166
    categorical, 122-124, 127, 132, 136-139
    continuous, 122-124, 127, 132, 136-139
Descriptive statistics, 128-130, 132, 133
Descriptive studies, 43
Discontinuous data, see Data Types, categorical
Discrete data, see Data Types, categorical
Discriminant analysis, 137-139, 142
Dissertation Abstracts, 25
Doctoral morals, complete listing of, 136-137

E

ERIC (Educational Resource Index Center), 16-23, 25
Experimental studies
    definition of, 43
    evaluation of, 44-47

F

Factor analysis, 138, 142-143
Findings, writing of, 194
Focus group, 112

G

Graphic techniques,
  for frequency distributions, 215, 216
  for descriptive statistics, 215, 217
  for inferential statistics, 218-226
  general, 215

H

Halo effect, 77, 89, 91
Hawthorne effect, 46, 89, 91
Homogeneity of variance, 135
Hypotheses
  and design relationship, 44, 53
  computerized testing commands, 174
  definitions of, 31
  directionality of, 34, 39-40
  writing of, 195
Hypotheses, types of
  alternate, 31, 33, 36-38
  alternative, 31, 33
  null, 31-32, 34-40, 195
  research, 31-33, 34-38

I

Inferential statistics, 132, 134, 136
Instruments, administration of
  by group interview, 110
  by mail interview, 110
  by telephone interview, 111
  by in-person interview, 112
Instruments, computer compatibility of, 155-156,
  158-163
Instrument items
  Likert-type, 79, 84-88
  multiple choice, 79-166
  readability of, 78
  response scales of, 78, 166
Interval data, see Data Types
Item analysis, 66, 68-72

J

Journal titles, 15-16

K-L

LERTAP, 68-72, 178-179
Limitations, writing of, 197
Listings of tables, illustrations, diagrams
  design of, 193
Literature review
  purpose of, 15
  writing of, 193

M

Mean
  standard error of, 133
  calculation of, 132-133
  definition of, 132
Measurement scales, 126, 137
Median, 132-133
Methods and procedures, writing of, 194
Mode, 132-133
Multiple regression, 137-139, 141

N

Nominal data, see Data Types
Non-statistical findings
  general, 224, 227-228
  writing of, 195
Null hypotheses
  and alpha levels, 145-147
  and statistical significance, 145-147
  rejecting, accepting, testing, 39-40
  see also Hypotheses

O

One-tail test, see Hypotheses, directionality of
Ordinal data, see Data Types

P

Parametric assumptions, 134-136, 140-143
Pearson correlation
  general, 137-141
  summary table, 182
  see also Correlation Coefficients

Pilot testing, 78, 90-95
Population
    definition of, 99
    diversity of, 104
    listings of, 104
    prior knowledge of, 104
    sizes of, 104
Practice effect, 45
Preliminary ideas, pro/con sheets, 3-7
Pro/Con preliminary idea sheets, see Preliminary Ideas
Problem statements, writing of, 193
Psychological abstracts, 16
Publication of documents, 8
Published test instruments, selection of, 72-76

Q-R

Ratio data, see Data Types
Recommendations, writing of, 197
References, quantity of, 25-26
References and bibliographies
    general, 225
    writing of, 198
References and suggested readings, rationale of, xviii
Reliability of test instruments
    equivalent forms, 63-65
    general, 60, 62, 80, 82, 91
    Hoyt's, 64-65
    internal consistency, 64-65
    split-half, 63, 65
    test-retest, 62, 65
Replication, 1, 121-122
Report presentation
    preparation of, 231-232
    dress during, 232
    overview of, 232
    outline for, 234-235
Report writing
    general, 187
    outline, 188-199
    styles, 199
Research
    designs, 47
    ideas, final workable, 3-7
    ideas, preliminary, 1-3

Respondents
   definition of, 99
   differences in, 104

S

Sample size
   adequacy, 101
   costs, 104
   definition, 99
   determination, 105, 113, 115-117
   per group, minimum, 136
   sub-sampling, 112
Sampling
   cluster, 102-104, 109
   convenience, 103
   definition of, 99
   general, 99, 105, 109, 115
   miscellaneous types of, 103
   quota, 103
   random, 100-101, 109
   simple random, see Sampling, random
   snowball, 103
   stratified, 101-102, 104, 109
   systematic, 100, 109
Self-fulfilling prophecy, 89, 91
Significance, statistical, 134
Sociological abstracts, 16
SPSS, see Statistical Package for the Social Sciences
Spearman's rho, 144-145
Standard deviation, 132-133
Standard error of the mean, see Mean
Statistical analysis, general, 121-122
Statistical Package for the Social Sciences (SPSS)
   as textbook, 175
   example of program, 175-177
   use in programming, 175
Statistical tests
   parametric, 134-139
   non-parametric, 134-139
Student's t-test, see t-Test

Index

T

t-Test
  general, 136-137, 140
  graphics for, 219-222
Table of contents, design of, 193
Time allotments, in research, 8
Title page, design of, 191
Turabian writing style, 199
Two-tail test, <u>see</u> Hypotheses, directionality of

U

Unhypothesized findings
  computerized testing commands, 174
  writing of, 195

V

Validity, of instruments
  concurrent, 57, 61
  construct, 60-61
  content, 55-57, 61, 78
  criterion-related, 57-59, 71
  experimental designs and, 47
  general, 53-61, 80, 83, 91
  predictive, 57, 61
Variables
  input format of, 178
  number in computer analysis, 165
  types in computer program, 165
Verb tenses, 225

W-Z

Worksheets, xvii
Writing
  format rules of, 224-225
  outline form for, 188-190

About the Author

Edward S. Balian received the Doctor of Philosophy and Master of Education degrees in Educational Evaluation and Research at Wayne State University, Detroit, Michigan.

Teaching graduate and undergraduate levels in areas of research methods, statistical analysis, computer use, and technical writing, Dr. Balian is currently an Assistant Professor at Madonna College, Livonia, Michigan. Additionally, as Director of Research Consulting, Incorporated, he has had extensive experience in all phases of conducting public and private research from educational, business, social and medical fields. Recently, Dr. Balian has also developed innovative educational software for micro-computers.

How to Design, Analyze and Write Doctoral Research was originally formulated from Dr. Balian's numerous private doctoral dissertation seminars. Additionally, through individualized instruction, Dr. Balian has helped hundreds of doctoral and masters candidates successfully complete their research efforts.

The author is sincerely interested in hearing from those using the text. Please write in care of the publisher.